# **200 more** one pot meals

hamlyn | all color cookbook

# 200 more one pot meals

Joanna Farrow

An Hachette UK Company
www.hachette.co.uk

First published in Great Britain in 2013 by Hamlyn
a division of Octopus Publishing Group Ltd
Endeavour House, 189 Shaftesbury Avenue
London, WC2H 8JY
www.octopusbooksusa.com



Distributed in the US by Hachette Book Group USA
237 Park Avenue, New York, NY 10017 USA

Distributed in Canada by Canadian Manda Group
165 Dufferin Street, Toronto, Ontario, Canada M6K 3H6



ISBN: 978-0-600-62673-2

Printed and bound in China

1 2 3 4 5 6 7 8 9 10

Standard level spoon and cup measurements are used in all recipes.

Ovens should be preheated to the specified temperature—if using a convection oven, follow the manufacturer's instructions for adjusting the time and temperature. Broilers should also be preheated.

Fresh herbs should be used unless otherwise stated.

Large eggs should be used unless otherwise stated.

Some of the recipes in this book have previously appeared in other titles published by Hamlyn.

People with known nut allergies should avoid recipes containing nuts or nut derivatives, and vulnerable people should avoid dishes containing raw or lightly cooked eggs.

# contents

# introduction

# introduction

When it comes to easy, fuss-free food, you can't do better than cooking one-pot meals. These include a feast of delicious dishes, from warming, wintry casseroles and stews to lighter soups, risottos and baked vegetables. As the term implies, the whole dish is cooked in one pot or dish, usually starting with browning or sautéing meat, vegetables, or fish, then adding various other ingredients and cooking the dish slowly and gently in order to let the flavors mingle and develop. The preparation is easy and there's little cleaning up involved and cooking times are flexible, too—most one-pot dishes will still be fine if left in the oven for longer than planned.

## equipment

Invest in sturdy, durable utensils for one-pot cooking and they will help contribute to your one-pot successes. Here are a few items you might want to consider buying if you don't already have them.

**flameproof casseroles**

These are the most useful of all the one-pot utensils, and they feature in many of the recipes in this book. Preparation usually starts on the stove using techniques such as browning or sautéing vegetables and meat, before adding other ingredients as well as transferring the pot to the oven. Flameproof casserole dishes with ovenproof handles are available in various sizes, and most are stylish enough to take from oven or stove to table. If you don't have pans that can be used both on the stove and in the oven, first use a skillet on the stove, then transfer the fried ingredients into an ovenproof casserole dish to finish cooking in the oven.

**saucepans**

A good-quality, heavy saucepan is a good investment and won't buckle, and the ingredients will be less likely to burn in the pan during cooking. Its efficient heat conduction means that you can leave the pan on the back burner without the risk of ingredients sticking to the bottom. A sturdy, heavy saucepan with double ovenproof handles for easy grip makes a good substitute for a flameproof casserole.

### sauté pans

These wide, shallow pans are deeper than skillets and are useful for recipes where you are gently browning meat or sautéing fish before adding stock, wine, or other liquids. A large, deep-sided skillet makes a good substitute because the contents can be stirred without slopping over the sides of the pan.

### skillets

Several of the recipes are cooked in a large, heavy skillet that enables you to sauté or brown ingredients and incorporate plenty of other ingredients. Some have lids, but you can use aluminum foil, secured around the rim of the pan, or a baking sheet instead.

### woks

These are great for simmering, steaming, and deep-frying as well as stir-frying. They have a rounded bottom designed to encourage the heat to encircle the whole pan and cook quickly and evenly. They are also great for recipes where your regular skillet is not quite large enough to incorporate all of the ingredients. Choose a wok with a completely round bottom for a gas stove or one with a slightly flattened bottom for an electric stove.

### baking dishes

Where a one-pot recipe is assembled in a dish without the need to first sauté or brown any ingredients, a shallow baking dish that can be taken directly to the table is useful.

### roasting pans

These pans have to endure high temperatures, both in the oven and on the stove; therefore, a good-quality one that doesn't buckle or burn is essential. Some of the recipes require a large pan so that the ingredients have space to roast and color. Opt for the largest size available that will comfortably fit in your oven.

### immersion blenders

Also known as stick or handheld blenders, these are great for blending soups in the pan you have cooked them in, saving time and effort in cleaning up. A food processor or blender can be used instead.

## techniques

There are certain simple techniques that are used repeatedly in one-pot cooking that you may not be familiar with. The following are worth knowing to produce successful results.

**browning meat**

Thoroughly browning ingredients, particularly meat and poultry, is one of the most crucial elements of successful one-pot cooking. The process develops a good flavor and adds a rich color to stews, casseroles, and pot roasts. First, make sure the meat is thoroughly dry, if necessary pressing it between several sheets of paper towels, then season and/or flour the pieces (see below). Heat the fat in the flameproof casserole or skillet and add some of the meat, spreading the pieces so that each has space around it. Don't add too many pieces at once, or the meat will steam in its own juices. Cook the pieces, shaking the pan gently but without turning them, until deep brown on the underside. Using a wooden spatula, turn the pieces until browned all over, then drain with a slotted spoon while you cook the next batch. Sometimes whole pieces of meat or poultry are seared in a pan before pot roasting. Use the same process, slowly turning the meat in the fat, not forgetting to sear the ends. In many recipes, butter is combined with oil for browning. The butter provides plenty of flavor; the oil prevents the butter from burning.

**flouring meat**

Sometimes meat is floured before cooking. This adds color but is ultimately used to thicken the juices of a stew or casserole as it cooks. Season the flour (as stated in the recipe) with salt and black pepper on a plate and turn the meat in the flour with your fingers until coated. Don't discard any excess flour left on the plate—transfer it to the pan when browning and it will help thicken the juices.

### skinning tomatoes

Tomato skins don't soften, even when cooked for some time, so are worth removing. Pull away the stems, make a slit with a knife, and put the tomatoes in a heatproof bowl. Cover with boiling water and let stand for about 30 seconds if the tomatoes are very ripe, or a couple of minutes if very firm. Drain and fill the bowl with cold water. Peel away the skins and halve or chop the tomatoes as required.

### crushing spices

A small coffee or spice grinder is ideal for crushing spices in seconds. A mortar and pestle makes a more traditional method of crushing spices, or you can use a small bowl and the end of a rolling pin. Lay a dish towel over the spices to stop the seeds from bouncing out. Don't spend time crushing seeds to a powder—a light pounding suffices.

### cutting up a chicken or other poultry

A few of the recipes in this book require a cut-up chicken or other poultry, which may not be available to buy. Follow these simple steps to cut up, or disjoint, your own. It's a useful skill to have and the bones can be kept to make stock (see page 36).

1 Cut vertically down through the skin and flesh between the leg and breast on one side of the bird. Pull the leg away from the body until the ball-and-socket joint at the carcass end of the thigh is exposed. Bend the leg back so that the joint snaps apart, then use the tip of the knife to release the meat around the joint. Remove the leg on the other side in the same way.
2 To make the wing portions meatier, a small piece of breast meat can be removed with them. Hold the wing and make a diagonal cut down through the back of the breast.

2 Feel around for the wing joint with the knife to locate the socket. Cut through this and remove the wing completely. Repeat on the other side.
3 Now, cut vertically down one side of the breastbone. Keeping the knife against the rib cage to avoid wasting any meat, pull the breast meat back with one hand as you ease the flesh away from the ribs with a knife. Repeat on the other side.
4 Place one of the legs, skin side down, on the board. Bend the leg so that you can see where the joint is located. (There is usually a thin piece of white fat over the joint where you need to aim the knife.) Cut down through this to divide the leg into two pieces. Repeat with the other leg.
5 Cut each breast across into two pieces.

## ingredients

Choose good-quality ingredients and you are halfway to making the perfect one-pot meal. Keep your pantry stocked with a supply of rice, lentils, beans, oils, spices, flavorings, and condiments, and buy the best fresh ingredients you can.

### meat

Beef should be a deep dark red, sometimes almost purple, with a marbling of fat running through the lean meat. These threadlike traces of white fat help keep the meat moist and succulent. The surface fat should be a creamy color, and both fat and

lean should look dry, not wet. Look for "dry-aged" beef that will have been aged naturally. Lamb should also be very red, although the color will depend more on the age of the lamb. Pork fat should look whiter and the flesh rosy pink, again with no wateriness. When buying chops and cutlets, look for ones of a similar thickness so that they cook evenly. Bone ends should be neatly sawn, not splintered, and rolled joints should be professionally and neatly tied. Avoid buying cuts from which all the fat has been trimmed off, because it's the fat that provides so much flavor and succulence while the meat cooks.

**fish**

Choose whole fish with bright, plump eyes instead of sunken dried ones. The fish should have a glossy, fresh sheen and plumpness as though they have only just been caught. The bodies should be firm with bellies intact instead of split (which might be an indication of staleness), particularly on oily fish. Fillets should look moist and succulent with flesh that holds together firmly. Avoid dull, ragged, dry-looking pieces. Oily fish, such as mackerel, sardines, and herrings, will deteriorate quickly, so be particularly careful when choosing these fish.

## Essential herbs

**Basil** Highly fragrant and aromatic, delicate basil leaves are best removed from their stems and coarsely chopped or torn into dishes toward the end of cooking. Used mainly in Mediterranean dishes, particularly tomato-based ones.

**Bay** These hardy leaves are added to one-pot dishes at the beginning of cooking because the flavor takes a while to emerge, but are removed afterward because they shouldn't be digested whole. Bay combines well with parsley and thyme and is used in slow-cooked meaty dishes.

**Chives** Has a mild onion flavor and are useful for adding a fresh burst of flavor to summery stews and casseroles as well as salad accompaniments. Finely chop or snip the leaves with scissors. Particularly good in fish, chicken, and vegetable dishes.

**Cilantro** Easily confused with flat leaf parsley, cilantro has more rounded, delicate leaves. Chop both the leaves and stems into spicy dishes. Use plenty for sprinking on top, too, because its aroma really stimulates the appetite.

**Dill** Delicate, feathery leaves resemble fennel tops with a mild licorice flavor. Discard any thick stems and chop the rest into fish and vegetable dishes.

**Oregano** Hardy oregano leaves are best removed from their stems and finely chopped into meat, chicken, or vegetable one-pot dishes. Widely used in Greek or Italian dishes, dried oregano is widely used.

**Parsley** Both "curly" and "flat leaf," or "Italian," varieties are indispensible in meat, fish, and vegetable one-pot dishes. Both stems and leaves can be used.

**Rosemary** Pull the needle-like leaves from the stems and finely chop for adding to dishes, or use the whole sprigs. Use chopped rosemary sparingly. Particularly good with lamb dishes.

**Sage** Green, variegated, and purple varieties are all used, either chopped or whole. Sage is good with meat dishes, in particular pork, and vegetables dishes.

**Tarragon** Delicate, spindle tarragon leaves have a mild licorice flavor and should be pulled from their stems and chopped into chicken, pork, fish, and vegetable dishes.

**Thyme** The many varieties of thyme are all useful in almost all slow cooked one-pot dishes. The tiny leaves of hardy thyme should be pulled from their stems and added at the beginning of cooking while the tender, young stems can be chopped and added later on.

### herbs: fresh & frozen

One of the most appetizing ingredients to add to any dish, herbs can be used liberally, with their fragrant, aromatic flavors mingling with and complementing almost any meat, fish, or vegetable dish. Hardier herbs, such as bay, thyme, and rosemary, are usually added to a dish early on in the cooking process, whereas more delicate herbs are stirred in at the end. Frozen herbs are a useful standby, particularly delicate ones, such as chives, tarragon, fennel, and dill. If you have bought too many fresh ones or have a bumper crop, chop them and freeze in bags for later use.

### oils

Most of the recipes use olive oil for sautéing, which is appropriate for Mediterranean dishes. Some olive oils are steeped with flavors such as basil, garlic, and chile. These are also good for sautéing, though chili oil is best used sparingly, because some brands are very hot. Other recipes require a vegetable oil such as sunflower, corn, or peanut oil. A couple of Asian dishes use stir-fry or wok oil. These are seasoned with flavors such as garlic and ginger, although you can use an ordinary vegetable oil instead. Flavored oils are easy to make yourself and are worth doing when you've got herbs left over from a recipe or plentiful supplies in the garden. Use a single herb or combine several in one oil. Use a light olive oil or sunflower oil as the base. Pack herbs, such as rosemary, basil, thyme, bay, oregano, or tarragon, into a bottle. Several cloves of garlic or pared strips of lemon can also be added. Fill the bottles with oil. Let stand in a cool place for several weeks, shaking often. Strain the oil into a clean bottle, adding fresh herb sprigs for presentation (especially if making as a present). Store in a cool place. For homemade chili oil, see page 216.

### Garlic

If you're not a fan of garlic, it can be left out of a one-pot recipe. If you love it, then be really generous. Garlic keeps well in the refrigerator but will gradually stale, so check before use; it should be firm and juicy, not dry and graying.

Garlic presses are good for crushing but using a board and sharp knife is quick and easy and saves on cleaning up. To crush by hand, press the side of a large knife firmly down on a clove with the heel of your hand. This detaches the skin and softens the flesh. Peel away the skin and chop the clove to break it up. Continue to crush the garlic by mashing it onto the board with the side of the knife. A little salt sprinkled over the garlic as you work will help break it down and stop the knife sliding around.

**Fresh ginger root**

Hot and fragrant, fresh root ginger is an invaluable addition to one-pot meals, particularly Asian and Indian dishes. Choose plump roots that are not too knobbly for easy peeling. Cut away knobbly areas that are difficult to peel, then use a vegetable peeler or scrape the ginger with the edge of a teaspoon to remove the skin. For most recipes, finely chop or grate the ginger, working over a plate to catch the delicious juices to add to the dish.

**Saffron**

Expensive but exotic, saffron is indispensible in certain fish and spiced dishes, including a classic paella. It can be crumbled directly into the pan or steeped in boiling water first to release its flavor. Crumble with your fingers into a small heatproof bowl. Add a tablespoon of boiling water and let stand for several minutes so the flavors can develop. Use both strands and liquid.

**Wine**

Both red and white wine make delicious additions to one-pot dishes from hearty meat and game dishes to lighter fish or vegetable ones. As a general rule, use an inexpensive wine (but one that you would drink). In most cases, it's red wine for meat and game and white wine for chicken and fish. If you've got some leftover wine that needs using up, you can add it to a one-pot dish in place of an equal measure of stock.

**spices**

A good store of spices adds plenty of variety to one-pot cooking but will deteriorate over time.

Check any that you have had stored for a while—if they have lost their spicy aroma, or simply have no aroma at all, throw them away. For most recipes, it's best to buy whole seeds such as cumin, coriander, fennel, and cardamom, and grind them yourself (see page 11).

### stock

A flavor-packed stock is essential to so many one-pot dishes, whether fish, meat, poultry, or vegetable. There are now some good-quality powdered stocks that make great pantry standbys, as well as liquid concentrates and store-bought prepared stocks. Some of these are vacuum packed and don't need refrigeration, while those from the refrigerator section will last several days. The best option is to make your own when fresh or cooked bones are available. It takes just a few minutes to get the stock pot going, and the rest takes care of itself. Once made, all cooled, strained stocks can be frozen in airtight containers or freezer bags for up to six months. See the individual recipes for homemade stock: chicken, page 36; beef, page 108; lamb, page 110; vegetable, page 210.

### tomato paste

A pantry essential, tomato paste is an intense tomato concentrate that adds flavor and color to various dishes. If you can find sun-dried tomato paste, it has a sweeter flavor and is perfect for Mediterranean dishes.

## accompaniments

The recipes in this book are designed to be complete dishes. To satisfy hungry appetites, a well-flavored bread warmed through before the dish is ready is the most effortless accompaniment to one-pot dining. It makes a delicious vehicle for mopping up the juices. Alternatively, a dish of creamy mashed potato or buttery greens make great partners to a wintry stew. A mixed or leafy green salad is an easy accompaniment. Store-bought cooked rice and noodles make useful standbys and are easy to reheat. Stir into a dish before serving. Couscous and bulgur wheat make fuss-free accompaniments for North African or Middle Eastern dishes.

# poultry & game

# chicken mole

Serves **4**
Preparation time **25 minutes**
Cooking time **1½ hours**

3 tablespoons **vegetable oil**
1 **chicken**, about 3 lb, cut up into pieces (see page 12)
1 **onion**, chopped
1 **green bell pepper**, cored, seeded and chopped
½ teaspoon **ground allspice**
½ teaspoon **ground cinnamon**
½ teaspoon **ground cumin**
1 teaspoon **chili powder**
2 **garlic cloves**, crushed
¾ cup **can diced tomatoes**
1¼ cups **chicken stock** (see page 38 for homemade)
1 store-bought or homemade corn **tortilla**, torn into pieces
⅓ cup **blanched almonds**, coarsely chopped
2 tablespoons **sesame seeds**, plus extra for sprinkling
½ ounce **bittersweet chocolate**, coarsely chopped
**salt** and **black pepper**
chopped **fresh cilantro**, to garnish

**Heat** the oil in a flameproof casserole and sauté the chicken pieces for 5 minutes, until golden on all sides. Transfer to a plate. Add the onion and green bell pepper to the casserole and sauté gently for 5 minutes, until softened, stirring in the spices and garlic for the last few minutes.

**Add** the tomatoes and half the stock and bring to a boil. Return the chicken to the pan, cover, and cook in a preheated oven, at 350°F, for 45 minutes.

**Meanwhile,** put the tortilla into a food processor with the almonds and sesame seeds. Process until finely ground. Pour in the remaining stock and process again until smooth. Stir the almond mixture and chocolate into the casserole and return to the oven for 30 minutes, until the chicken is cooked through and tender.

**Season** to taste with salt and black pepper, then sprinkle with extra sesame seeds and sprinkle with chopped cilantro to garnish. Serve with warm tortillas, if liked.

**For homemade corn tortillas**, mix together 2 cups masa harina corn flour and ½ teaspoon salt in a bowl. Add 1 tablespoon lemon juice and 1 cup lukewarm water and mix to a dough, adding a dash more water if the dough feels dry. Knead into a smooth dough and let stand, covered with plastic wrap, for 30 minutes. Divide the dough into 8 pieces and shape into small balls. Roll out each dough ball on a lightly floured surface. Heat a dry skillet or flat griddle and cook the tortillas for about 1 minute on each side or until beginning to color. Serve immediately or wrap in aluminum foil and reheat in a preheated oven, at 350°F, for 15 minutes.

# pot-roasted pheasant with croutons

Serves **5–6**
Preparation time **10 minutes**, plus soaking
Cooking time **2 hours**

¾ oz **mixed dried mushrooms**
1¼ cups **boiling water**
2 **pheasants**
3 tablespoons **butter**
2 tablespoons **vegetable oil**
4 oz **smoked bacon**, chopped
2 **small onions**, chopped
2 **small parsnips**, diced
2 **garlic cloves**, crushed, plus 1 **plump garlic clove**, peeled
1 tablespoon **all-purpose flour**
1¼ oz **red wine**
1 tablespoon **chopped thyme**
1 small **French bread**
2 tablespoons **red currant jelly** or **apple jelly**
**salt** and **black pepper**

**Place** the dried mushrooms in a heatproof bowl and pour the water over them. Let soak for 10 minutes.

**Rinse** the pheasants and pat dry with paper towels. Season with salt and black pepper.

**Melt** the butter with the oil in a large flameproof casserole and sauté the pheasants, one at a time, for 5 minutes, until golden on all sides, then transfer to a plate. Add the bacon, onions, parsnips, and garlic to the casserole and sauté for 5 minutes. Sprinkle in the flour and cook, stirring, for 1 minute. Remove from the heat and blend in the wine, then stir in the mushrooms and their soaking liquid and the thyme. Bring to a simmer, stirring.

**Return** the pheasants to the casserole, nestling them into the vegetables. Cover and cook in a preheated oven, at 300°F, for 1¾ hours or until the pheasants are cooked through. Meanwhile, cut the bread into thin slices and toast on both sides. Halve the garlic clove and rub the cut sides over the toast.

**Transfer** the pheasants to a board or carving platter, cover with aluminum foil, and keep warm. Add the red currant or apple jelly to the casserole and stir until melted. Season to taste with salt and black pepper. Carve the pheasants and pile the meat onto the croutons on warm serving plates. Spoon the vegetables and gravy on top.

**For chicken & sausage pot roast**, make the recipe as above using a 3½ lb chicken instead of the pheasants and omitting the parsnips. Skin and chop 8 oz Italian-style sausages and add to the casserole with the mushrooms and thyme. Replace the red currant jelly with 2 tablespoons grape jelly.

# lemon chile chicken

Serves **4**
Preparation time **25 minutes**, plus marinating
Cooking time **45 minutes**

1 **chicken**, about 3½ lb, cut up into pieces (see page 12)
8 **garlic cloves**, peeled
4 **juicy lemons**, quartered and squeezed, peels reserved
1 **small red chile**, seeded and chopped
2 tablespoons **orange blossom honey**
¼ cup **chopped parsley**, plus sprigs to garnish
**salt** and **black pepper**

**Arrange** the chicken pieces in a shallow flameproof dish. Crush 2 of the garlic cloves and add them to the lemon juice with the chile and honey. Stir well, then pour the mixture over the chicken. Tuck the lemon peels around the meat, cover, and let marinate in the refrigerator for at least 2 hours or overnight, turning once or twice.

**Turn** the chicken pieces skin side up, sprinkle with the remaining whole garlic cloves, and place the lemon peels, cut side down, on top.

**Cook** the chicken in a preheated oven, at 400°F, for 45 minutes or until golden brown, cooked through, and tender. Stir in the chopped parsley, season to taste with salt and black pepper, and serve garnished with parsley sprigs.

**For cilantro rice & peas**, to serve as a side dish, bring a large saucepan of lightly salted water to a boil and add 1⅓ cups white long-grain rice, then reduce the heat and simmer for about 15 minutes, or according to the package directions, until tender. Drain well. Meanwhile, cook 1⅔ cups frozen peas in a separate saucepan of lightly salted boiling water for about 3 minutes. Drain and toss with 4 tablespoons melted butter, 2 chopped scallions, and a handful of chopped fresh cilantro. Fork the pea mixture into the cooked rice.

# rabbit & mushroom risotto

Serves **4**
Preparation time **25 minutes**
Cooking time **40 minutes**

5 tablespoons **butter**
2 cups sliced **cremini mushrooms**
8 oz **boneless lean rabbit**, diced
1 **onion**, chopped
1 **celery stick**, diced
3 **garlic cloves**, crushed
1 teaspoon finely **chopped thyme**
300 g (10 oz) **risotto rice**
1 1/4 cups **red wine**
3 1/3 cups **hot chicken stock** (see page 36 for homemade)
1/4 cup **chopped parsley**
**salt** and **black pepper**

**Melt** 1 tablespoon of the butter in a large saucepan and sauté the mushrooms for about 5 minutes, until lightly browned. Lift out with a slotted spoon onto a plate and set aside.

**Season** the rabbit lightly with salt and black pepper. Melt another 1 tablespoon of the butter in the pan and sauté the rabbit for 5 minutes, until beginning to brown. Add the onion and celery and sauté gently, stirring frequently, for about 5 minutes, until the vegetables have softened.

**Stir** in the garlic, thyme, and rice and cook, stirring, for 1 minute. Add the wine and cook quickly until the wine has been absorbed. Gradually add the hot stock to the pan, a ladleful at a time, and cook, stirring frequently, until each ladleful has mostly been absorbed before adding the next. This should take 20–25 minutes, by which time the rice should be tender but retaining a little bite and the consistency should be creamy. You may not need all the stock.

**Return** the mushrooms to the pan and stir in the remaining butter and the parsley. Season to taste with salt and black pepper and serve immediately.

**For chicken, blue cheese & thyme risotto**, make the risotto as above, omitting the mushrooms sautéed in butter and using 8 oz diced boneless, skinless chicken instead of the rabbit and 2/3 cup white wine in place of the red wine. Once the risotto is cooked, crumble 1 cup blue cheese over the top instead of using the remaining butter and stir through until melted.

# Cornish game hens with walnuts

Serves **4**
Preparation time **20 minutes**
Cooking time **1½ hours**

4 **Cornish game hens**
4 tablespoons **butter**
1 tablespoon **olive oil**
⅔ cup chopped **walnuts**
3 **zucchini**, thickly sliced
1 **large onion**, chopped
3 **garlic cloves**, chopped
⅔ cup **chicken stock** (see page 36 for homemade)
1 tablespoon **tarragon leaves**
½ cup **sour cream**
**salt** and **black pepper**

**Rinse** the Cornish game hens and pat dry with paper towels. Season all over with salt and black pepper. Melt half the butter with the oil in a large flameproof casserole and sauté the walnuts for a couple of minutes, until beginning to color. Lift out with a slotted spoon onto a plate. Add the zucchini to the casserole and sauté for about 5 minutes, until lightly browned on both sides. Lift out onto the plate and set aside.

**Melt** the remaining butter in the casserole and sauté the onion for 2 minutes. Add the Cornish game hens and sauté for 5 minutes, until golden on all sides. Add the garlic and stock and bring to a boil. Cover with a lid or aluminum foil and cook in a preheated oven, at 350°F, for 45 minutes. Add the tarragon leaves to the casserole with the walnuts and zucchini, then return to the oven for another 30 minutes.

**Lift** the Cornish game hens from the pan onto warmed serving plates. Drain the walnuts and zucchini onto the plates with a slotted spoon. Stir the sour cream into the sauce and bring to a boil. Check the seasoning, then spoon onto the plates. Serve with bread or mashed potatoes, if liked.

**For Cornish game hens with tomatoes & pine nuts**, replace the walnuts with ⅓ cup pine nuts and sauté in the butter, then set aside as above. Omit the zucchini and sauté the onion, then sauté the Cornish game hens and garlic as above. Add 1 (14½ oz) can diced tomatoes, 1 teaspoon granulated sugar, and 3 tablespoons tomato paste with the stock. Cook in the oven as above, adding 3 tablespoons chopped oregano and the pine nuts for the final 30 minutes of cooking time.

# turkey & ham casserole

Serves **6**
Preparation time **20 minutes**
Cooking time **1 hour 45 minutes**

- 12 oz **cooked ham** in one piece
- 2 tablespoons **all-purpose flour**
- 1¼ lb **turkey breast meat**
- 4 tablespoons **butter**
- 2 **onions**, chopped
- 2 **celery sticks**, sliced
- 3 cups **chicken stock** (see page 36 for homemade)
- 1 tablespoon **chopped thyme**
- ½ teaspoon **mild chili powder**
- 2 **sweet potatoes**, scrubbed and cut into small chunks
- 1½ cups **cranberries**
- ½ cup **crème fraîche** or **sour cream**
- **salt** and **black pepper**

**Cut** the ham into dice. Season the flour with a little salt and black pepper on a plate. Cut the turkey into small chunks and coat with the seasoned flour.

**Melt** the butter in a flameproof casserole and sauté the turkey for 5 minutes, until golden on all sides. Add the onions and celery to the casserole and sauté for 4–5 minutes, until softened. Tip in any remaining flour left on the plate. Blend in the stock, add the thyme and chili powder and bring to a simmer, stirring.

**Cover** the casserole and cook in a preheated oven, at 350°F, for 45 minutes.

**Stir** the sweet potatoes and ham into the casserole and return to the oven for another 30 minutes. Stir in the cranberries and crème fraîche or sour cream and season to taste with salt and black pepper. Return to the oven for a final 15 minutes before serving.

**For turkey, ham & mushroom pie**, trim and slice 8 oz button mushrooms (about 3½ cups). Make the recipe as above, lifting the turkey and vegetables out with a slotted spoon onto a plate after sautéing. Sauté the mushrooms in another 1 tablespoon of butter before returning the turkey and vegetables to the casserole. Cook as above, omitting the sweet potatoes but adding the ham. Let cool. Roll out 1 sheet ready-to-bake puff pastry, thawed if frozen, on a lightly floured surface to the same diameter as the casserole dish and rest the pastry over the filling. (If the casserole dish is too big, transfer the filling to a pie plate.) Brush with beaten egg to glaze and bake in a preheated oven, at 400°F, for 40 minutes or until the pastry is deep golden.

# slow-roasted duck & red currants

Serves **4**
Preparation time **25 minutes**
Cooking time **2 hours 15 minutes**

4 large **duck legs**
3/4 teaspoon **ground cinnamon**
8 **red-skinned** or **white round potatoes** (2 lb), peeled and cut into 3/4 inch dice
2 **turnips**, cut into thin wedges
8 **garlic cloves**, peeled but left whole
1 tablespoon **coarsely chopped thyme**
1 cup **red currants** or **grapes**
2/3 cup **chicken stock** (see page 36 for homemade)
3 tablespoons **red currant jelly** or **grape jelly**
1/4 cup **crème fraîche** or **sour cream**
**salt** and **black pepper**

**Halve** the duck legs by cutting each through the joints. Mix the cinnamon with a little salt and black pepper and rub over the duck legs. Arrange in a large roasting pan and roast in a preheated oven, at 300°F, for 1 1/4 hours.

**Drain** off most of the fat in the roasting pan, leaving just enough to coat the vegetables. Increase the oven temperature to 400°F.

**Add** the potatoes, turnips, garlic, and thyme to the roasting pan, turning them in the oil and seasoning lightly with salt and black pepper. Return the roasting pan to the oven for 45 minutes, until the vegetables are deep golden, turning frequently. Meanwhile, remove the red currants from the stems by passing the stems between the tines of a fork.

**Transfer** the duck legs and vegetables to warm serving plates and keep warm. Drain off the excess fat in the roasting pan, leaving the meaty juices. Add the stock, red currant or grape jelly, and crème fraîche and bring to a boil on the stove. Cook until slightly reduced and thickened. Stir in the red currants or grapes, season to taste with salt and black pepper, and heat for 1 minute. Spoon the sauce over the duck to serve.

**For buttered beans & zucchini**, to serve as an accompaniment, steam 2 cups trimmed green beans for 5 minutes, until tender. Add 1 large thickly sliced zucchini and steam for 2 minutes. Turn into a warm serving dish and add 3 tablespoons butter, 3 tablespoons chopped chives, 2 tablespoons chopped parsley, and a little salt and black pepper. Stir until the butter has melted and serve hot.

# chicken mulligatawny

Serves **6**
Preparation time **20 minutes**
Cooking time **1½ hours**

4 tablespoons **butter**
1¼ lb **bone-in, skinless chicken thighs**
2 **onions**, chopped
2 **small carrots**, chopped
1 **small Granny Smith** or **other cooking apple**, peeled, cored, and chopped
1 tablespoon **all-purpose flour**
4 cups **chicken stock** (see below for homemade)
2 tablespoons **mild curry paste**
2 tablespoons **tomato paste**
¼ cup **basmati** or **long-grain rice**
**plain yogurt**, for topping
**salt** and **black pepper**

**Melt** half the butter in a saucepan and sauté the chicken thighs in two batches for 5 minutes each, until golden on all sides. Lift out with a slotted spoon onto a plate. Add the remaining butter and sauté the onions, carrots, and apple, stirring, for 6–8 minutes, until lightly browned.

**Sprinkle** in the flour and cook, stirring, for 1 minute. Gradually blend in the stock, then stir in the curry paste, tomato paste, and rice. Return the chicken to the pan and bring to a simmer, stirring. Reduce the heat, cover, and cook gently for 1 hour, until the chicken is cooked through and tender.

**Lift** the chicken pieces from the pan. Once cool enough to handle, pull the meat from the bones. Shred half the meat into pieces and return the remainder to the pan. Blend the soup using an immersion blender or in a food processor.

**Return** the shredded chicken to the pan and heat through. Season to taste with salt and black pepper and serve in bowls topped with spoonfuls of plain yogurt.

**For homemade chicken stock**, place 1 large chicken carcass or 1 lb chicken bones in a large saucepan and add 2 halved, unpeeled onions, 2 coarsely chopped carrots, 1 coarsely chopped celery stick, several bay leaves, and 1 teaspoon black or white peppercorns. Just cover with cold water and bring to a gentle simmer. Reduce the heat to its lowest setting and cook, uncovered, for 2 hours. Strain through a fine strainer and let cool. Cover and store in the refrigerator for up to several days or freeze for up to 6 months.

# venison, stout & chestnut stew

Serves **6**
Preparation time **25 minutes**
Cooking time **2 hours 15 minutes**

3 tablespoons **all-purpose flour**
2½ lb **venison**, diced
4 tablespoons **butter**
8 ounces **pancetta** or **bacon**, chopped
1 **small leek**, trimmed, cleaned and chopped
3 **carrots**, diced
2 **parsnips**, diced
4 **garlic cloves**, crushed
2 teaspoons **chopped rosemary**
2 cups **stout**
1¼ cups **beef stock** (see page 108 for homemade)
2 cups **cooked peeled chestnuts**
1 lb **new potatoes**, scrubbed and cut into small chunks
**salt** and **black pepper**

**Season** the flour with salt and black pepper on a plate. Coat the venison with the flour.

**Melt** the butter in a flameproof casserole and sauté the venison, in batches, until browned, lifting out with a slotted spoon onto a plate. Add the pancetta or bacon, leek, carrots, and parsnips to the casserole and sauté gently for 6–8 minutes, until lightly browned. Add the garlic, rosemary, and any flour leftover from coating, and cook, stirring, for 1 minute.

**Blend** in the stout and stock and bring to a simmer, stirring. Return the venison to the casserole, then reduce the heat, cover, and cook very gently for 1½ hours or until the meat is tender.

**Add** the chestnuts and potatoes and cook for another 20 minutes or until the potatoes are cooked through. Season to taste with salt and black pepper.

**For pheasant, red wine & shallot stew**, put 10 oz shallots in a heatproof bowl, cover with boiling water, and let stand for 2 minutes. Drain and rinse in cold water. Peel away the skins, leaving the shallots whole. Make the recipe as above, using 2½ lb diced pheasant instead of the venison and adding the shallots when sautéing the vegetables. Then replace the stout with 2 cups red wine, 2 tablespoons tomato paste, and 1 tablespoon packed dark brown sugar, and omit the chestnuts.

# chicken with spring vegetables

Serves **4**
Preparation time **10 minutes**, plus resting
Cooking time about **1¼ hours**

1 **chicken**, about 3 lb
about 6⅓ cups **hot chicken stock** (see page 36 for homemade)
2 **shallots**, halved
2 **garlic cloves**, peeled but left whole
2 **parsley sprigs**
2 **marjoram sprigs**
2 **lemon thyme sprigs**
2 **carrots**, halved
1 **leek**, trimmed, cleaned, and sliced
8 oz **baby broccoli**
8 oz **asparagus spears**, trimmed
½ **savoy cabbage**, shredded
**crusty bread**, to serve

**Put** the chicken into a large saucepan and pour in enough stock just to cover the chicken. Push the shallots, garlic, herbs, carrots, and leek into the pan and bring to a boil, then reduce the heat and simmer gently for 1 hour or until the chicken is falling away from the bones.

**Add** the remaining vegetables to the pan and simmer for another 6–8 minutes or until the vegetables are cooked.

**Turn** off the heat and let rest for 5–10 minutes before serving the chicken and vegetables in deep bowls with spoonfuls of the broth. (Remove the chicken skin, if preferred.) Accompany with plenty of crusty bread.

**For Chinese chicken soup**, cook the recipe as above, replacing the shallots, herbs, carrots, and leek with a 3 inch piece of fresh ginger root, peeled and thinly sliced, 2 sliced garlic cloves, 1 teaspoon Chinese five-spice powder, 4–5 star anise, and ½ cup dark soy sauce. Then add 16 baby corn and 4 cups snow peas to the pan instead of the broccoli, asparagus, and cabbage and simmer for a few minutes, until just cooked before serving.

# duck with fruited bulgur wheat

Serves **4**
Preparation time **25 minutes**, plus marinating
Cooking time **25 minutes**

- 4 **duck breasts**, about 5–6 oz each
- 2 teaspoons **harissa paste**
- 2 teaspoons **coriander seeds**, crushed
- 2 **garlic cloves**, crushed
- 3 tablespoons **olive oil**
- 1 cup **bulgur wheat**
- 2½ cups **chicken stock** (see page 36 for homemade)
- ⅔ cup coarsely chopped **hazelnuts**
- ½ cup thinly sliced **dried apricots**
- 1½ cups thinly sliced **snow peas**
- 2 tablespoons **pomegranate molasses**
- 2 teaspoons packed **dark brown sugar**
- seeds of 1 **pomegranate**
- **salt** and **black pepper**

**Use** a small sharp knife to score several deep cuts through the skin side of each duck breast and place in a shallow, nonmetallic dish. Mix together the harissa, coriander, and garlic and spread all over the duck breasts. Cover loosely and let marinate in the refrigerator for at least 30 minutes, up to several hours.

**Scrape** the marinade off the duck breasts and reserve. Heat 1 tablespoon of the oil in a large heavy skillet, add the duck breasts, skin side down, and cook for 3–4 minutes or until the skin is deep golden. Turn and cook for another 2 minutes. Transfer to a plate.

**Add** the bulgur wheat, stock, and reserved marinade to the pan. Bring to a simmer, then reduce the heat, cover with a lid or aluminum foil, and cook gently for 5 minutes, until the bulgur wheat is softened. Stir in the hazelnuts and apricots and return the duck to the pan, pushing the breasts down into the bulgur wheat. Cook gently for another 8–12 minutes (or 15–20 minutes if you prefer the duck well cooked through). Add the snow peas to the pan once the duck is just cooked to your liking.

**Stir** the pomegranate molasses and sugar into the bulgur wheat, drizzle with the remaining oil, and add salt and black pepper. Serve topped with pomegranate seeds.

**For chicken & bulgur pilaf**, replace the duck with 4 chicken breasts cut horizontally in half to make 8 thin fillets. Marinate as above. Coarsely chop ⅔ cup pistachio nuts and 9 dried figs, discarding the hard stems. Cook the chicken as the duck, above, using the pistachio nuts and figs instead of hazelnuts and apricots, making sure the chicken is cooked through.

# cheese & eggplant chicken

Serves **4**
Preparation time **25 minutes**
Cooking time **50 minutes**

4 **boneless, skinless chicken breasts**, about 4–5 oz each
4 oz **Muenster** or **mozzarella cheese**
several **mint sprigs**, chopped
1/3 cup **olive oil**
1 **onion**, chopped
1 **fennel bulb**, trimmed and finely chopped
1 1/2 **eggplants**, cut into 3/4 inch chunks
3 **garlic cloves**, crushed
2 cups **chicken** or **vegetable stock** (see pages 36 and 208 for homemade)
1/3 cup **tomato paste**
1 teaspoon **dried oregano**
**salt** and **black pepper**

**Lay** the chicken breasts on a board. To create a large pocket for the stuffing, use a small sharp knife to make a horizontal cut in the center of each breast without cutting right through to the other side.

**Dice** the cheese into a bowl and stir in the mint and a little black pepper to season. Pack the mixture into the chicken breast pockets and secure in place with wooden toothpicks.

**Heat** 2 tablespoons of the oil in a large, heavy skillet and sauté the chicken breasts for 5 minutes, until golden on both sides. Transfer to a plate. Add another 2 tablespoons of the oil to the skillet and gently sauté the onion, fennel, and half the eggplants for 5 minutes, stirring, until lightly browned. Remove from the skillet. Sauté the remaining eggplants in the last of the oil for 5 minutes, adding the garlic once the eggplants have browned.

**Return** all the vegetables to the skillet and stir in the stock, tomato paste, and oregano. Bring to a simmer. Push the chicken breasts down into the eggplants and reduce the heat to its lowest setting. Cook for about 30 minutes, stirring frequently, until the chicken is cooked through and the eggplants are tender. Season to taste with salt and black pepper and serve.

**For basil & yogurt sauce**, to serve as a side dish, tear 2/3 cup basil leaves into small pieces. Mix together 1/2 cup Greek yogurt and 1/3 cup sour cream in a bowl with 1 crushed garlic clove, a squeeze of lemon juice, and the basil. Turn into a serving dish, cover with plastic wrap, and chill until ready to serve.

# guinea fowl & sausage stew

Serves **5–6**
Preparation time **20 minutes**
Cooking time **1¾ hours**

1 **guinea fowl**, about 2 lb, cut up into pieces (see page 12)
4 tablespoons **butter**
1 tablespoon **vegetable oil**
6 **pork link sausages**
2 **carrots**, sliced
2 **leeks**, trimmed, cleaned, and sliced
1½ tablespoons **all-purpose flour**
2 cups **chicken stock** (see page 36 for homemade)
⅔ cup **red wine**
1 teaspoon **juniper berries**, crushed with mortar and pestle
8 **red-skinned** or **white round potatoes** (2 lb)
**salt** and **black pepper**

**Season** the guinea fowl pieces on all sides. Melt half the butter with the oil in a shallow, flameproof casserole and sauté the guinea fowl pieces for 5 minutes, until golden on all sides. Transfer the meat to a plate and reserve. Sauté the sausages for 5 minutes, until browned all over. Transfer to a plate.

**Add** the remaining butter to the casserole and gently sauté the carrots and leeks for 5 minutes, until softened. Sprinkle in the flour and cook, stirring, for 1 minute. Remove from the heat and blend in the stock and wine. Stir in the juniper berries. Bring to a boil, stirring, then reduce the heat to a gentle simmer. Return the guinea fowl to the pan, cover, and cook gently for 30 minutes.

**Slice** the potatoes thinly and arrange over the top of casserole. Season to taste. Cover with the lid or aluminum foil and cook in a preheated oven, at 350°F, for 30 minutes. Dot the potatoes with the remaining butter and return to the oven for 30 minutes, until the potatoes are crisped and browned. (Put the dish under a preheated broiler for a few minutes, if desired.)

**For easy butter pastry**, as an alternative to the potato topping, put 2 cups all-purpose flour in a bowl and grate in 1¼ sticks butter, stirring it into the flour frequently so that it doesn't clump. Add 2 egg yolks and ⅓ cup cold water and mix with a blunt knife to a firm dough, adding a dash more water if the dough feels dry and crumbly. Wrap and chill for 30 minutes. Make the casserole as above, extending the initial cooking time to 50 minutes. Let cool, then cover with the rolled-out pastry. Brush with beaten egg and bake in a preheated oven, at 400°F, for 40 minutes, until the pastry is golden.

# chicken & sweet potato wedges

Serves **4**
Preparation time **20 minutes**
Cooking time **35 minutes**

4 **sweet potatoes** (2½ lb), scrubbed
4 **boneless, skinless chicken thighs**, cut into chunks
1 **red onion**, cut into wedges
4 **plum tomatoes**, cut into chunks
5 oz **chorizo sausage**, skinned and sliced or diced, depending on diameter
leaves from 3 **rosemary sprigs**
¼ cup **olive oil**
**salt** and **black pepper**

**Cut** the sweet potatoes in half, then into thick wedges and place in a large roasting pan with the chicken, onion, and tomatoes. Tuck the chorizo in and around the potatoes, then sprinkle with the rosemary and some salt and black pepper. Drizzle with the oil.

**Roast** in a preheated oven, at 400°F, for about 35 minutes, turning once or twice, until the chicken is golden and cooked through and the potato wedges are browned and tender.

**Spoon** onto warm serving plates and serve with a green salad, if desired.

**For mixed roots with fennel & chicken**, use a mixture of 2½ lb baking potatoes, parsnips, and carrots. Scrub the potatoes and peel the parsnips and carrots, then cut all the root vegetables into wedges. Add to the roasting pan with the chicken as above. Sprinkle with 2 teaspoons fennel seeds, 1 teaspoon ground turmeric, and 1 teaspoon paprika, then drizzle with ¼ cup olive oil and roast as above.

# turkey patties with tomatoes

Serves **4**
Preparation time **25 minutes**
Cooking time **30 minutes**

1 lb **ground turkey**
2 **onions**, chopped
1 (2 oz) **can anchovy fillets**, drained and chopped
1 cup **fresh white bread crumbs**
¼ cup **olive oil**
2 (14½ oz) **cans diced tomatoes**
2 tablespoons **tomato paste**
2 teaspoons **dried oregano**
1 tablespoon packed **light brown sugar**
4 oz **mozzarella cheese**, drained and thinly sliced
**salt** and **black pepper**

**Mix** together the turkey, one of the onions, the anchovies, bread crumbs, and a little salt and black pepper in a bowl. Divide the mixture into 8 pieces and shape into flat patties.

**Heat** 2 tablespoons of the oil in a large skillet and sauté the patties for 8 minutes, until golden on both sides. Transfer to a plate. Add the remaining oil and onion to the pan and sauté gently for 5 minutes. Stir in the tomatoes, tomato paste, oregano, sugar, and a little salt and black pepper and bring to a simmer.

**Return** the patties to the pan, pushing them down into the sauce. Cook gently, uncovered, for 15 minutes, until the patties are cooked through.

**Place** the mozzarella slices on top and season with plenty of black pepper. Cook under a preheated moderate broiler until the cheese melts. Serve with warm olive ciabatta, if liked.

**For chicken cutlets with tomatoes & olives**, halve 4 chicken breasts, about 4–5 oz each, horizontally and place the slices between 2 sheets of plastic wrap. Beat with a rolling pin to make thin cutlets. Season with salt and black pepper. Cook the recipe as above using the chicken cutlets in place of the turkey patties and sprinkling the tomato mixture with ½ cup chopped pitted black or green olives before adding the mozzarella.

# chicken, ham & cabbage stew

Serves **6**
Preparation time **30 minutes,** plus overnight soaking
Cooking time **2 hours 10 minutes**

1 **ham hock** or **cured ham,** about 1½ lb
¾ cup **dried navy beans**
4 **chicken legs**
2 **onions,** chopped
3 **bay leaves**
5 cups **cold water**
4 **red-skinned** or **white round potatoes**
1 tablespoon **ground paprika**
2 cups shredded **green cabbage**
⅓ cup coarsely chopped **fresh cilantro**
**black pepper**

**Soak** the ham and beans in separate bowls of cold water overnight.

**Drain** the beans and transfer to a large saucepan. Cover with fresh cold water and bring to a boil. Reduce the heat and simmer for 40 minutes or until just tender. Drain and set aside.

**Add** the drained ham to the empty bean pan with the chicken legs, onions, and bay leaves. Pour in the measured water and bring to a gentle simmer. Cover and cook gently for 1 hour.

**Cut** the potatoes into small chunks and add to the pan with the beans and paprika. Cook gently, covered, for another 20 minutes, until the potatoes are tender.

**Lift** the chicken and ham from the pan. Once cool enough to handle, pull the meat from the bones, discarding the skin. Shred or chop all the meat into small pieces and return to the pan. Stir in the cabbage and cilantro and heat through gently. Season with black pepper and serve.

**For hearty chicken broth**, soak and then cook the beans as above. Omitting the ham, cook 6 chicken legs with the onions and bay leaves as above, also adding 3 large chopped carrots and 1 teaspoon caraway seeds. Then add ¼ cup finely chopped parsley and a little salt with the potatoes, beans, and paprika, and continue as above.

# quails with lentils & spiced pears

Serves **4**
Preparation time **15 minutes**
Cooking time **1¼ hours**

12 **shallots**
2 teaspoons **ground ginger**
½ teaspoon **chili powder**
4 **plump quails**
3 tablespoons **butter**
1 tablespoon **olive oil**
2 **ripe pears**, cored and cut into wedges
1 cup **dried green lentils**
1 **cinnamon stick**, halved
2 cups **chicken stock** (see page 36 for homemade)
**salt**
**watercress**, to serve

**Place** the shallots in a heatproof bowl, cover with boiling water, and let stand for 2 minutes. Drain and rinse in cold water. Peel away the skins, leaving the shallots whole.

**Mix** together the ginger, chili powder, and a little salt and rub all over the quails. Melt the butter with the oil in a flameproof casserole and sauté the quails for 5 minutes, until browned on all sides. Transfer the quails to a plate.

**Add** the shallots and pears to the casserole, turning them in the butter for a few minutes, until beginning to color. Lift out the pears and set aside, then return the quail to the pan.

**Rinse** the lentils in cold water and pour around the quails. Add the cinnamon stick and stock and bring to a simmer. Cover and cook in a preheated oven, at 350°F, for 50 minutes, until the quails are cooked through and the lentils are tender.

**Stir** the pears into the lentils and return to the oven for another 10 minutes. Serve with salad greens.

**For creamy celeriac purée**, to serve as an accompaniment, cut away the skin from a large celeriac and chop into large dice. Cut 3 russet or Yukon gold potatoes into similar-size pieces. Put the vegetables into a large saucepan and cover with water. Season with a little salt and bring to a boil. Cook for about 20 minutes, until the vegetables are tender. Drain well and return to the pan. Add 4 tablespoons butter, ½ cup Greek yogurt, and plenty of black pepper and mash well with a potato masher until smooth.

# rabbit in white wine with rosemary

Serves **4–6**
Preparation time **15 minutes**
Cooking time **2 hours**

2 tablespoons **butter**
3 tablespoons **olive oil**
1 **rabbit**, about 3 lb, cut up into pieces
2 **onions**, thinly sliced
1 **small celery stick**, finely diced
pinch of **dried red pepper flakes**
3 **large rosemary sprigs**
1 **lemon**, quartered
12 **black olives**
1½ cups **dry white wine**
1 cup **chicken stock** (see page 36 for homemade)
**salt**

**Melt** the butter with the oil in a large flameproof casserole with a tight-fitting lid large enough to hold the rabbit in a single layer. Season the rabbit pieces lightly with salt and add to the casserole with the onions, celery, red pepper flakes, and rosemary. Cover, reduce the heat to its lowest setting, and cook for 1½ hours, turning the rabbit pieces every 30 minutes.

**Remove** the lid, increase the heat to high, and boil for 15 minutes, until most of the rabbit juices have evaporated. Add the lemon quarters and olives and stir well, then pour in the wine. Bring to a boil and boil for 2 minutes.

**Add** the stock and simmer, turning and basting the rabbit occasionally, for another 10–12 minutes, until the sauce is syrupy. Serve hot.

**For chicken with olives & rosemary**, replace the rabbit with 1 chicken, about 3 lb, cut up into pieces (see page 12). Place the chicken with all the remaining ingredients above in a large roasting pan and cook in a preheated oven, at 400°F, for 1 hour, turning the chicken pieces occasionally, until the chicken is cooked through and tender and most of the juices have evaporated. Stir in 3 tablespoons heavy cream and serve immediately.

# miso chicken broth

Serves **4**
Preparation time **10 minutes**
Cooking time **20 minutes**

1 tablespoon **sunflower oil**
2 **boneless, skinless chicken breasts**, diced
3½ cups sliced **button mushrooms**
1 **carrot**, cut into thin matchsticks
¾ inch **piece of fresh ginger root**, grated
2 large pinches of **dried red pepper flakes**
2 tablespoons **brown rice miso paste**
¼ cup **mirin** or **dry sherry**
2 tablespoons **light soy sauce**
5 cups **cold water**
2 **bok choy**, thinly sliced
4 **scallions**, thinly sliced
¼ cup **chopped fresh cilantro**

**Heat** the oil in a saucepan and sauté the chicken for 5 minutes, until golden on all sides. Add the mushrooms and carrot sticks, then the ginger, red pepper flakes, miso paste, mirin or sherry, and soy sauce.

**Pour** in the measured water and bring to a boil, stirring. Reduce the heat and simmer for 10 minutes.

**Add** the bok choy, scallions, and cilantro to the pan and cook for 2–3 minutes, until the bok choy has just wilted. Spoon into bowls and serve immediately.

**For hot & sour chicken soup**, sauté the chicken in the oil as above, then add 2 cups sliced mushrooms and 1 carrot, cut into matchsticks. Flavou with 2 finely chopped garlic cloves, 1 tablespoon red Thai curry paste, 1 tablespoon Thai fish sauce, and 2 tablespoons light soy sauce. Add 5 cups chicken stock, bring to a boil, and cook for 10 minutes. Add 8 sliced baby corn and 1 cup sliced snow peas with the scallions and cilantro as above and cook for 2–3 minutes. Ladle into bowls and serve with lime wedges.

# pigeon with bacon & spelt

Serves **2**
Preparation time **15 minutes**, plus marinating
Cooking time **40 minutes**

2 teaspoons **granulated sugar**
2 teaspoons **salt**
4 **pigeon breasts**
2 tablespoons **butter**
1 **onion**, chopped
4 **smoked bacon slices**, chopped
6 **tomatoes**, skinned (see page 11) and coarsely chopped
2 tablespoons **balsamic vinegar**
1¼ cups **chicken stock** (see page 36 for homemade)
½ cup **whole spelt**
¼ cup **basil leaves**, torn into pieces, plus extra to garnish
**salt** and **black pepper**

**Mix** the sugar with the salt and spread over the pigeon breasts. Put into a nonmetallic bowl, cover loosely, and let marinate in the refrigerator for 2–3 hours.

**Wipe** off the salt and sugar and pat the pigeon breasts dry with paper towels. Melt the butter in a large, heavy skillet and sauté the pigeon breasts for 5 minutes, until lightly browned on both sides. Transfer the pigeon to a plate and set aside.

**Add** the onion and bacon to the skillet and sauté gently for about 5 minutes, until the bacon begins to crisp.

**Stir** in the tomatoes, vinegar, stock, and spelt and bring to a boil. Reduce the heat, cover, and cook gently for 25 minutes or until the spelt is just tender.

**Cut** the pigeon into slices, add to the skillet with the basil and a little salt and black pepper and heat through. Serve sprinkled with extra basil.

**For pigeon with pickled walnut pilaf**, marinate the pigeon breasts in the sugar and salt, then sauté in the butter and lift out onto a plate as above. Sauté the onion in the pan as above, adding ¼ cup slivered almonds and 2 crushed garlic cloves instead of the bacon. Add ⅔ cup white long-grain rice, 1 cup chicken stock, ¼ teaspoon ground allspice, and 3 tablespoons raisins. Cover and cook gently for 15–20 minutes, until the rice is tender, adding a dash of water if the stock has been absorbed before the rice is cooked. Return the sliced pigeon to the pan with 3 chopped pickled walnuts (available online) and 3 tablespoons chopped fresh cilantro. Season to taste with salt and black pepper and serve.

# chicken, chorizo & black bean stew

Serves **4–5**
Preparation time **15 minutes**, plus overnight soaking
Cooking time **2¼ hours**

- 1⅓ cups **dried black beans**
- 8 **bone-in, skinless chicken thighs**
- 5 oz **chorizo sausage**, cut into small chunks
- 1 **onion**, sliced
- 1 **fennel bulb**, trimmed and chopped
- 2 **green bell peppers**, cored, seeded, and cut into chunks
- 1 teaspoon **saffron threads**
- **salt** and **black pepper**

**Soak** the beans in a bowl of cold water overnight. Drain, rinse, and transfer to a large flameproof casserole. Cover with plenty of fresh cold water. Bring to a boil and boil for 10 minutes. Drain the beans, rinse, and return to the pan.

**Add** the chicken, chorizo, onion, fennel, and green bell peppers and sprinkle in the saffron. Almost cover the ingredients with cold water and bring to a simmer. Cover and cook in a preheated oven, at 325°F, for 2 hours or until the beans are soft.

**Drain** a couple of spoonfuls of the beans with a large slotted spoon to a bowl and mash with a fork. Return to the casserole, stirring gently to thicken the juices. Season to taste with salt and black pepper and serve.

**For chorizo with chickpeas**, sauté 5 oz diced chorizo in a large saucepan. Add 2 thinly sliced shallots, 2 (14½ oz) cans diced tomatoes, 2 (15 oz) cans chickpeas, ¼ cup raisins, 2 tablespoons sherry vinegar, 1 tablespoon honey, and 1 teaspoon ground paprika. Bring to a simmer, then reduce the heat, cover, and cook gently for 30 minutes. Season to taste with salt and black pepper and serve.

# venison & pork meatballs

Serves **4**
Preparation time **30 minutes**
Cooking time **1½ hours**

12 oz **ground venison**
8 oz **ground pork**
2 teaspoons **chopped thyme**
3 tablespoons **olive oil**
1 **onion**, chopped
3 **carrots**, chopped
1 tablespoon **all-purpose flour**
1 cup **beef stock** (see page 108 for homemade)
1¼ cups **red wine**
3 tablespoons **tomato paste**
3 **bay leaves**
1 lb **new potatoes**, scrubbed
**salt** and **black pepper**

**Place** the ground venison and pork, thyme, and a little salt and black pepper in a bowl and mix until well combined. Shape into 12 small balls about 1¼ inches in diameter.

**Heat** 2 tablespoons of the oil in a large, heavy skillet and sauté the meatballs, half at a time, for 8–10 minutes, until browned on all sides, and lift out with a slotted spoon onto a plate.

**Add** the remaining oil to the skillet with the onion and carrots. Cook gently for 6–8 minutes, until the vegetables have softened. Sprinkle in the flour and cook, stirring, for 1 minute. Remove from the heat and blend in the stock and wine. Stir in the tomato paste and bay leaves.

**Bring** to a boil, stirring, then reduce the heat to its lowest setting, cover with a lid or aluminum foil, and cook gently for 10 minutes. Add the potatoes and meatballs to the pan, replace the lid, and cook for another 50 minutes, until the potatoes and meatballs are cooked through and tender. Check the seasoning and serve.

**For merguez-spiced meatballs with butternut squash**, make and sauté the meatballs as above, adding 2 teaspoons each lightly crushed cumin, coriander seeds, and fennel seeds and 2 teaspoons ground paprika instead of the thyme. Make the sauce as above, omitting the wine and using 2 cups beef stock. Replace the new potatoes with ½ butternut squash, skinned, seeded, and diced, and add 1 cup sliced dried figs, and ¼ cup chopped fresh cilantro with the meatballs.

# chicken with spring herbs

Serves **4**
Preparation time **15 minutes**
Cooking time **25 minutes**

8 oz **mascarpone cheese**
1 handful of **chervil**, finely chopped
½ bunch of **parsley**, finely chopped
2 tablespoons **chopped mint leaves**
4 **boneless, skin-on chicken breasts**
2 tablespoons **butter**
1 cup **white wine**
**salt** and **black pepper**

**Mix** together the mascarpone and herbs in a bowl and season well with salt and black pepper. Lift the skin away from each chicken breast and spread one-quarter of the mascarpone mixture on each breast. Replace the skin and smooth carefully over the mascarpone mixture. Season with salt and black pepper.

**Place** the chicken in a baking dish, dot with the butter, and pour the wine around it.

**Roast** the chicken in a preheated oven, at 350°F, for 20–25 minutes, until golden and crisp and cooked through. Serve with garlic bread, if liked.

**For baby glazed carrots**, to serve as an alternative accompaniment to the garlic bread, melt 2 tablespoons butter in a saucepan, add 1 lb young carrots, quartered lengthwise, a pinch of granulated sugar, and season with salt and pepper to taste. Pour in just enough water to cover and simmer gently for 15–20 minutes, until the carrots are tender and the liquid has evaporated, adding 2 tablespoons orange juice toward the end of the cooking time. Serve with the chicken garnished with chopped parsley.

# meat

# lamb with fava beans & fennel

Serves **4**
Preparation time **10 minutes**
Cooking time **2¾ hours**

2 lb **lamb cutlets**
1 cup **fresh white bread crumbs**
2 small **fennel bulbs**, trimmed and cut into thin wedges
1 ⅓ cups **shelled fava beans**
finely grated rind of 1 **lemon,** plus 1 tablespoon **juice**
⅓ cup **chopped parsley**, plus extra to garnish
4 **garlic cloves**, crushed
3 tablespoons **extra virgin olive oil**
½ cup **dry white wine** or **chicken stock** (see page 36 for homemade)
2 tablespoons **molasses**
**salt** and **black pepper**

**Cut** the lamb into 2 inch lengths, discarding any areas of excess fat. Put into a large bowl and add the bread crumbs, fennel, fava beans, lemon rind, parsley, and garlic. Mix the ingredients together well and transfer to a casserole.

**Mix** the olive oil with the wine or stock, lemon juice, and molasses and drizzle the mixture over the meat.

**Cover** the casserole and cook in a preheated oven, at 400°F, for 45 minutes.

**Reduce** the oven temperature to at 325°F. Turn the ingredients in the casserole, replace the lid, and return to the oven for another 2 hours. Season to taste with salt and black pepper and serve sprinkled with extra parsley. Serve with warmed olive ciabatta, if liked.

**For cannellini & mashed potatoes**, to serve as an alternative accompaniment to the ciabatta, cook 4 russet or Yukon gold potatoes in a saucepan of lightly salted boiling water until tender. Drain, reserving a ladleful of the cooking water. Return the potatoes to the pan with the reserved water and 2 (15 oz) cans cannellini beans, drained, and 1 tablespoon chopped young thyme leaves. Mash well with a potato masher until smooth. Beat in ⅓ cup extra virgin olive oil and serve hot.

# spiced steak & bell pepper wraps

Serves **6**
Preparation time **20 minutes,** plus marinating
Cooking time **25 minutes**

1 ½ lb **skirt steak** or **top sirloin steak**
1 teaspoon **dried oregano**
2 teaspoons **cumin seeds**
2 teaspoons **granulated sugar**
2 **garlic cloves**, crushed
finely grated rind and juice of 1 **lime**
¼ cup **vegetable oil**
2 **red onions,** thinly sliced
2 **red bell peppers**, cored, seeded, and thinly sliced
2 **orange** or **yellow bell peppers**, cored, seeded, and thinly sliced
6 **wheat tortillas**, warmed
2 **Boston lettuce**, shredded

**To serve**
**sour cream**
**sweet chili sauce**

**Cut** the beef into ½ inch-wide strips, discarding any areas of excess fat. Place in a nonmetallic bowl.

**Crush** the oregano and cumin seeds using a mortar and pestle and mix with the sugar, garlic, and lime rind and juice. Add to the beef and mix until well combined. Cover loosely and let marinate in the refrigerator for 1 hour.

**Heat** the oil in a skillet or wok and sauté the onions and bell peppers, stirring frequently, for 20 minutes, until soft and beginning to brown. Drain the vegetables to a plate and wipe out the pan. Sauté the beef, in batches, in the remaining oil until browned on all sides, adding the cooked meat to the plate as you sauté the remaining meat. Return the bell peppers, onions, and beef to the pan and heat through briefly. Add any marinade left in the bowl and cook, stirring, for about 5 minutes.

**Serve** wrapped in the warm tortillas with the lettuce, along with sour cream and sweet chili sauce.

**For avocado relish**, to serve as an additional accompaniment, pit and peel 2 ripe avocados, then finely chop. Skin (see page 11) and scoop the seeds from 2 small tomatoes, then finely chop the flesh. Mix in a bowl with the avocado, 1 finely chopped scallion, the finely grated rind and juice of 1 lime, 2 teaspoons granulated sugar, 3 tablespoons finely chopped fresh cilantro, and a little salt and black pepper. Stir together and transfer to a serving dish.

# pork & leek stew with dumplings

Serves **4–5**
Preparation time **25 minutes**
Cooking time **2 hours**

2 lb **boneless lean pork**, diced
2 tablespoons **vegetable oil**
1 large **onion**, chopped
5–6 **leeks**, trimmed, cleaned and chopped
3 **bay leaves**
6⅓ cups **beef** or **chicken stock** (see pages 108 and 36 for homemade)
⅓ cup **pearl barley**
1¼ cups **all-purpose flour**
1 teaspoon **baking powder**
⅓ cup **beef suet** or **vegetable shortening**
about ½ cup **cold water**
1 cup halved **pitted prunes**
**salt** and **black pepper**

**Season** the pork with salt and black pepper. Heat 1 tablespoon of the oil in a large flameproof casserole and sauté the pork, in batches, until browned on all sides, lifting out with a slotted spoon onto a plate. Add the remaining oil to the casserole and gently sauté the onion and leeks for 5 minutes.

**Return** the pork to the casserole, add the bay leaves and stock, and bring to a simmer. Stir in the pearl barley. Cover, reduce the heat to its lowest setting, and cook for about 1½ hours, until the pork and barley are tender and the cooking juices have thickened.

**Mix** together the flour, baking powder, suet or shortening, and a little salt and black pepper in a bowl. Add the measured water and mix with a blunt knife to a soft dough, adding a dash more water if the mixture feels dry and crumbly, but don't make it too sticky.

**Stir** the prunes into the stew and season to taste with salt and black pepper. Using a tablespoon, place spoonfuls of the dumpling mixture on the surface of the stew, spacing them slightly apart. Replace the lid and cook gently for 15–20 minutes, until the dumplings have risen and have a fluffy texture. Serve in bowls.

**For Irish mashed potatoes**, to serve as an alternative accompaniment to the dumplings, cook 10 russet or Yukon gold potatoes (2½ lb) in a large saucepan of lightly salted boiling water until tender. Drain, return to the pan, and mash with a potato masher until smooth. Finely chop 1 bunch of scallions and add to the pan with 4 tablespoons butter, 1 cup milk, and plenty of black pepper. Beat well, check the seasoning, and serve.

# oxtail stew with star anise

Serves **4**
Preparation time **20 minutes**
Cooking time **3¾ hours**

2 tablespoons **all-purpose flour**
4 lb **oxtail**
3 tablespoons **vegetable oil**
2 **onions**, chopped
2 **celery sticks**, chopped
5 **star anise**
¼ cup peeled and finely chopped **fresh ginger root**
3⅓ cups **beef** or **chicken stock** (see pages 108 and 36 for homemade)
¾ cup **can diced tomatoes**
finely grated rind and juice of 1 **orange**
2 tablespoons **soy sauce**
¼ cup **chopped fresh cilantro**, plus extra to garnish
**salt** and **black pepper**

**Season** the flour with salt and black pepper on a plate. Coat the oxtail with the flour.

**Heat** the oil in a flameproof casserole and sauté the oxtail, in batches, until browned on all sides, lifting out with a slotted spoon onto a plate. Add the onions and celery to the casserole and sauté gently for 5 minutes. Add the star anise, ginger, and any flour leftover from coating, and cook, stirring, for 1 minute.

**Blend** in the stock, tomatoes, orange rind and juice, and soy sauce. Return the oxtail to the pan and bring to a simmer, stirring. Cover and cook in a preheated oven, at 300°F, for about 3½ hours or until the meat falls easily from the bone.

**Fold** in the cilantro and season to taste with salt and black pepper. Serve garnished with extra cilantro.

**For beery oxtail stew**, make the stew as above, adding 2 chopped carrots when sautéing the vegetables and omitting the star anise and ginger. Replace half the stock with 2 cups strong ale and the tomatoes, orange, soy sauce, and cilantro with ¼ cup tomato paste, 2 tablespoons molasses, 2 tablespoons Worcestershire sauce, and ¼ cup chopped parsley.

# beef, pickled onion & beer stew

Serves **4**
Preparation time **10 minutes**
Cooking time **2¼ hours**

3 tablespoons **all-purpose flour**
2 lb **chuck shoulder steak**
2 tablespoons **olive oil**
1 lb **pickled onions, drained**
2 **carrots**, thickly sliced
1¼ cups **beer**
2½ cups **beef stock** (see page 108 for homemade)
¼ cup **tomato paste**
1 tablespoon **Worcestershire sauce**
2 **bay leaves**
**salt** and **black pepper**
**chopped parsley**, to garnish

**Season** the flour with salt and black pepper on a plate. Cut the beef into large chunks and coat with the flour.

**Heat** the oil in a large flameproof casserole and sauté the beef, in batches, until browned on all sides, lifting out with a slotted spoon onto a plate. Return all the beef to the casserole.

**Stir** the pickled onions and carrots into the casserole, then gradually blend in the beer and stock. Bring to a boil, stirring, then add the tomato paste, Worcestershire sauce, bay leaves, and salt and black pepper to taste.

**Cover** and cook in a preheated oven, at 325°F, for 2 hours, stirring halfway through, until the beef and vegetables are tender. Garnish with chopped parsley and serve immediately.

**For soft Parmesan polenta**, to serve as an accompaniment, bring 4 cups water to a boil with 2 teaspoons salt in a saucepan. Add 1¼ cups polenta or cornmeal in a stream, beating constantly to prevent lumps from forming. Once it starts to thicken, use a wooden spoon to stir the polenta while it cooks for 5 minutes. Remove from the heat and stir in 4 tablespoons butter and ¼ cup freshly grated Parmesan cheese. Season to taste with salt and black pepper and serve immediately.

# veal with orzo

Serves **4**
Preparation time **15 minutes**
Cooking time **25 minutes**

1 1/4 lb **veal cutlets**
1/4 cup **olive oil**
1 large **onion**, finely chopped
4 **garlic cloves**, crushed
4 **ripe tomatoes**, skinned (see page 11) and coarsely chopped
3 cups **chicken stock** (see page 36 for homemade)
1 cup **tomato puree**
1/4 cup **tomato paste**
2 tablespoons **finely chopped oregano**
8 oz **dried orzo pasta**
2/3 cup crumbled **feta cheese**
**salt** and **black pepper**

**Cut** the veal cutlets into pieces about 2 inches across. Season on both sides with salt and black pepper.

**Heat** the oil in a flameproof casserole and quickly sauté the veal pieces, in two batches, for 5 minutes, until lightly browned on both sides, lifting out with a slotted spoon onto a plate. Add the onion to the casserole and sauté gently for 5 minutes, until softened. Stir in the garlic and sauté for 1 minute.

**Add** the tomatoes to the casserole with the stock, tomato puree, tomato paste, and oregano. Bring to a boil and stir in the orzo. Reduce the heat and cook, stirring frequently, for 6–8 minutes, or according to the package directions, until the pasta has softened.

**Return** the veal to the casserole and season to taste with salt and black pepper. Cook for 2 minutes. Sprinkle the feta over the meat before serving.

**For garlic & saffron alioli**, to serve as an alternative accompaniment to the feta topping, place 1/2 teaspoon crumbled saffron threads in a bowl with 1 tablespoon boiling water. Let stand for 2 minutes. Crush 1 plump garlic clove and mix with 1/2 cup mayonnaise in a separate bowl. Stir in the saffron and liquid and season lightly with salt and black pepper. Turn into a small bowl and serve spooned over the veal.

# irish lamb & potato stew

Serves **4–5**
Preparation time **20 minutes**
Cooking time **2¾ hours**

2 lb **lamb chops** or **lamb cutlets**
2 tablespoons **vegetable oil**
6 **carrots**, sliced
3 **onions**, chopped
1 **leek**, trimmed, cleaned, and thinly sliced
6 **russet** or **Yukon gold potatoes**, cut into large chunks
3 **bay leaves**
¼ cup **pearl barley**
4 cups **lamb** or **chicken stock** (see pages 110 and 36 for homemade)
¼ cup **chopped parsley**
¼ cup **chopped chives**
**salt** and **black pepper**

**Cut** the lamb into chunky pieces and season with salt and black pepper.

**Heat** the oil in a flameproof casserole or large saucepan and sauté the lamb, in batches, until browned on all sides, lifting out with a slotted spoon onto a plate.

**Layer** the lamb, carrots, onions, leek, and potatoes in the pan. Add the bay leaves and sprinkle in the pearl barley.

**Pour** the stock over all the ingredients and bring to a simmer. Cover, reduce the heat to its lowest setting, and cook for 2½ hours or until the lamb is meltingly tender.

**Stir** in the parsley and chives and cook for another 10 minutes. Season to taste with salt and black pepper and serve.

**For lamb stew with spring vegetables**, sauté the lamb, then layer in the casserole or saucepan with the onions, leek, and potatoes, cover with the stock, and cook for 2 hours as above. Stir in 12 oz scrubbed baby carrots, 1⅓ cups shelled baby fava beans, and 2 tablespoons chopped mint, then replace the lid and cook for another 30 minutes. Finally, add 10 trimmed asparagus spears and cook for another 5 minutes.

# mediterranean pork casserole

Serves **2**
Preparation time **10 minutes**
Cooking time **1 hour 10 minutes**

1 tablespoon **olive oil**
8 oz **boneless lean pork**, cut into chunks
1 **red onion**, cut into thin wedges
1 **garlic clove**, crushed
1 **yellow bell pepper**, cored, seeded, and chopped
8 **artichoke hearts in oil**, drained and quartered
¾ cup **canned diced tomatoes**
1 small glass **red wine**
½ cup **black olives**
grated rind of 1 **lemon**
1 **bay leaf**
1 **thyme sprig**, plus extra to garnish
**garlic bread,** to serve

**Heat** the oil in a flameproof casserole and sauté the pork for 4–5 minutes, until browned on all sides. Lift out with a slotted spoon onto a plate.

**Add** the onion, garlic, and yellow bell pepper to the casserole and sauté for 2 minutes. Return the pork to the casserole along with all the remaining ingredients.

**Bring** to a boil, then reduce the heat, cover, and cook gently for 1 hour or until the meat is tender. Garnish with thyme and serve with garlic bread.

**For cranberry bean casserole**, omit the pork and sauté the onion, garlic, and yellow bell pepper in the oil as above, then stir in the artichoke hearts and tomatoes. Rinse and drain 1 (15 oz) can cranberry beans and add to the casserole with the wine, olives, lemon rind, and herbs. Bring to a boil, then reduce the heat, cover, and cook gently for about 1 hour. Serve garnished with chopped parsley.

# Greek lamb & potato casserole

Serves **4**
Preparation time **15 minutes**
Cooking time **2 hours 5 minutes**

8 **lamb loin chops**
1 tablespoon **olive oil**
2 **onions**, thinly sliced
2 tablespoons **chopped oregano**
finely grated rind and juice of 1 **lemon**
1 **cinnamon stick**, halved
2 **tomatoes**, skinned (see page 11) and thinly sliced
1 lb **new potatoes**, halved or quartered
⅔ cup **lamb** or **chicken stock** (see pages 110 and 36 for homemade)
**salt** and **black pepper**
**Greek bread**, to serve

**Season** the chops on both sides with salt and black pepper. Heat the oil in a shallow, flameproof casserole with a tight-fitting lid and sauté the chops for 5 minutes, until browned on both sides.

**Sprinkle** the onions into the casserole and add the oregano, lemon rind and juice, and cinnamon. Tuck the tomatoes and potatoes around the lamb and add the stock and a little salt and black pepper.

**Cover** and bake in a preheated oven, at 325°F, for 2 hours or until the lamb is tender. Serve with warm Greek bread.

**For lamb chili with potatoes**, heat 2 tablespoons olive oil in a saucepan and sauté 1 lb ground lamb with 1 chopped onion, 1 teaspoon crushed cumin seeds, and ½ teaspoon dried red pepper flakes, breaking up the meat with a wooden spoon, for 8 minutes, until lightly browned. Add 1 (14½ oz) can plum tomatoes, 2 teaspoons packed light brown sugar, and 2 cups lamb or chicken stock. Bring to a simmer, then reduce the heat, cover, and cook gently for 15 minutes. Stir in a drained (15 oz) can red kidney beans, 1⅔ cups scrubbed and diced new potatoes, and 3 tablespoons chopped fresh cilantro. Replace the lid and cook for another 25 minutes or until the potatoes are tender. Check the seasoning and serve.

# liver & caramelized onions

Serves **4**
Preparation time **10 minutes**
Cooking time **40–45 minutes**

4 tablespoons **butter**
2 tablespoons **olive oil**
2 **large onions**, thinly sliced
1 1/4 1b **liver**, thinly sliced (ask your butcher to slice as thinly as possible)
2 tablespoons finely chopped **flat leaf parsley**
**salt** and **black pepper**

**Melt** half the butter with the oil in a large, heavy skillet with a tight-fitting lid. Add the onions and season with salt and black pepper, then cover, reduce the heat to its lowest setting, and cook, stirring occasionally, for 35–40 minutes, until soft and golden.

**Lift** the onions out with a slotted spoon into a bowl and increase the heat under the skillet to high.

**Season** the liver with salt and black pepper. Melt the remaining butter in the skillet. Once the butter starts foaming, add the liver and cook for 1–2 minutes, until browned. Turn over and return the onions to the skillet. Cook for another 1 minute. Serve sprinkled with the parsley.

**For chicken livers & caramelized onions**, cook the onions as above and lift from the skillet. Instead of the calf liver, use 12 oz chicken livers. Season 2 tablespoons all-purpose flour with salt and black pepper on a plate and coat the livers with the flour. Cook the livers in the remaining butter in the skillet as above for 4–5 minutes, turning once. Add 1 tablespoon aged balsamic vinegar and swirl in the skillet for a couple of seconds, then return the caramelized onions to the skillet. Cook for another 1 minute, then stir in the parsley as above and serve immediately.

# pork cheek mushroom casserole

Serves **5–6**
Preparation time **20 minutes**
Cooking time **2¾ hours**

3 tablespoons **all-purpose flour**
2 lb **pork cheeks**
4 tablespoons **butter**
1 tablespoon **vegetable oil**
5 cups sliced **cremini mushrooms**
2 **onions**, chopped
1½ cups **hard cider** or **apple juice**
1¼ cups **pork** or **chicken stock** (see page 36 for homemade)
2 tablespoons chopped **tarragon**
2 tablespoons **whole-grain mustard**
¼ cup **heavy cream**
**salt** and **black pepper**

**Season** the flour with salt and black pepper on a plate. Cut the pork cheeks into chunks and coat with the flour.

**Melt** half the butter with the oil in a flameproof casserole and sauté the pork, in batches, until browned on all sides, lifting out with a slotted spoon onto a plate. Melt the remaining butter in the casserole and sauté the mushrooms for 5 minutes, until all their juices have evaporated and they are pale golden. Lift out onto a separate plate and set aside.

**Return** the pork to the casserole with any flour leftover from coating and cook, stirring, for 1 minute. Stir in the onions, then blend in the cider or apple juice and stock. Bring to a boil, stirring, then cover and cook in a preheated oven, at 300°F, for 2½ hours or until the meat is tender, adding the tarragon and mustard halfway through cooking.

**Return** the mushrooms to the casserole and stir in the cream. Heat through gently, season to taste with salt and black pepper, and serve.

**For beef & ale casserole**, cut 2 lb chuck shoulder steak into large pieces, discarding any areas of excess fat. Make the casserole as above using the beef instead of the pork and 1½ cups strong ale in place of the cider. Add the mustard with 1 tablespoon chopped thyme instead of the tarragon, then finish with the cream as above.

# lamb stew with lima beans

Serves **4**
Preparation time **15 minutes**
Cooking time **1¼ hours**

1½ lb **lamb cutlets**
¼ cup **olive oil**
2 **red onions**, thinly sliced
2 **garlic cloves**, crushed
1 teaspoon **ground turmeric**
1 teaspoon **ground ginger**
1 teaspoon **ground cinnamon**
⅔ cup **lamb** or **chicken stock** (see pages 110 and 36 for homemade)
2 tablespoons **honey**
2 store-bought or homemade **preserved lemons** (see below)
1 cup **pitted ripe black olives**
2 (15 oz) **cans lima beans**, rinsed and drained
¼ cup **chopped parsley**, plus extra to garnish
**salt** and **black pepper**

**Cut** the lamb into 2 inch pieces, discarding any areas of excess fat. Season with salt and black pepper.

**Heat** the oil in a flameproof casserole and sauté the lamb, half at a time, until browned on all sides, lifting out with a slotted spoon onto a plate. Add the onions to the casserole and sauté for 5 minutes, until softened. Add the garlic and spices and cook, stirring, for 1 minute.

**Stir** the stock and honey into the casserole and bring to a simmer. Return the lamb to the pan, cover, and cook in a preheated oven, at 325°F, for 40 minutes.

**Meanwhile,** halve the preserved lemons and discard the pulp. Finely chop the rind.

**Add** the preserved lemon rind to the casserole with the olives, beans, and parsley. Return to the oven for another 20 minutes. Season to taste with salt and black pepper, garnish with extra parsley, and serve with warm flatbreads, if liked.

**For homemade preserved lemons**, wash and dry 3 small unwaxed lemons. Cut lengthwise into 8 wedges, keeping them intact at one end. Measure 3 tablespoons sea salt and sprinkle the cut sides of the lemons with 2 tablespoons of the measured salt. Pack the lemons into a thoroughly clean canning jar in which they fit snugly. Tuck a couple of bay leaves into the jar and add the remaining salt. Squeeze the juice from another 2 lemons and pour into the jar. Top up with cold water until the lemons are completely covered. Tap the jar to remove any air bubbles. Store at room temperature for a couple of days, then store in the refrigerator for a least 2 weeks before use; use within 6 months.

# pork chops baked with potatoes

Serves **4**
Preparation time **10 minutes**
Cooking time **50 minutes**

2 tablespoons **olive oil**
4 **large pork chops**, about 8 oz each
4 oz **smoked bacon**, diced
1 **large onion**, sliced
6 red-skinned or white round **potatoes**, peeled and cut into 1 inch cubes
2 **garlic cloves**, chopped
2 teaspoons **dried oregano**
grated rind and juice of 1 **lemon**
1 cup **chicken stock** (see page 36 for homemade)
**salt** and **black pepper**
**thyme leaves**, to garnish

**Heat** the oil in an ovenproof skillet or flameproof casserole and sauté the pork chops until browned on both sides. Lift out with a slotted spoon onto a plate.

**Add** the bacon and onion to the pan and cook over medium heat, stirring, for 3–4 minutes, until golden.

**Stir** the potatoes, garlic, oregano, and lemon rind into the pan. Pour in the stock and lemon juice and season lightly with salt and black pepper. Cook, uncovered, in a preheated oven, at 350°F, for 20 minutes.

**Arrange** the chops on top of the potato mixture and return to the oven for another 20 minutes or until the potatoes and pork chops are cooked through. Serve garnished with thyme leaves.

**For pork chops with roasted sweet potatoes & sage**, cook the recipe above using 4 sweet potatoes, peeled and cut into cubes, instead of the potatoes, and 1 tablespoon chopped sage in place of the dried oregano.

# beef, beet & red cabbage

Serves **6**
Preparation time **25 minutes**
Cooking time **2¾ hours**

2 teaspoons **black pepper**
2 tablespoons **all-purpose flour**
2 lb **skirt steak**
2 tablespoons **olive oil**
4 oz **bacon**, chopped
2 **onions**, sliced
1 ¼ cups **red wine**
1 ¼ cups **beef stock** (see page 108 for homemade)
¼ cup **tomato paste**
2 teaspoons **caraway seeds**
8 **beets**, scrubbed and cut into thin wedges
¾ small head **red cabbage**, sliced
3 tablespoons **balsamic vinegar**
**salt**
**sour cream** and **whole-grain bread**, to serve

**Mix** the black pepper into the flour with a little salt on a plate. Cut the steak into large chunks, about 2 inches across, and coat with the flour.

**Heat** 2 tablespoons of the oil in a flameproof casserole and sauté the beef, in batches, until browned on all sides, lifting out with a slotted spoon onto a plate.

**Add** the bacon and onions to the casserole and sauté gently for 6–8 minutes, until beginning to brown. Add any flour leftover from coating and cook, stirring, for 1 minute.

**Blend** in the wine and stock, then return the steak to the pan with the tomato paste and caraway seeds. Bring to a simmer, stirring, then cover and cook in a preheated oven, at 300°F, for 1 hour.

**Stir** the beets, red cabbage, and balsamic vinegar into the casserole and return to the oven for another 1 ½ hours or until the steak and vegetables are tender. Add a little salt, if necessary, and serve in bowls with sour cream and warmed whole-grain bread.

**For creamy horseradish mashed potatoes**, to serve as an accompaniment, cook 10 russet or Yukon gold potatoes (2 ½ lb) in a large saucepan of salted boiling water for 20 minutes or until tender. Drain and return to the pan. Dot 4 tablesppons butter into the potatoes with ½ cup crème fraîche or heavy cream and ¼ cup hot horseradish sauce. Mash well with a potato masher until smooth.

# asian pork with water chestnuts

Serves **4**
Preparation time **20 minutes**, plus marinating
Cooking time **10 minutes**

1 lb **pork tenderloin**
⅓ cup **soy sauce**
1 teaspoon **Chinese five-spice powder**
2 tablespoons **honey**
1 teaspoon **cornstarch**
3 tablespoons **cold water**
2 tablespoons **vegetable oil**
3 cups shredded **bok choy**
1 bunch of **scallions,** cut into ¾ inch lengths
¾ inch piece of **fresh ginger root**, peeled and finely chopped
1 **hot red chile**, seeded and thinly sliced
3 **garlic cloves**, thinly sliced
⅔ cup drained and halved **canned water chestnuts**
10 oz **prepared fine noodles**

**Cut** the pork tenderloin in half lengthwise, then across into thin slices, discarding any areas of excess fat. Put into a bowl and drizzle with 2 tablespoons of the soy sauce, the five-spice powder, and honey. Mix well, cover, and marinate in a cool place for 30 minutes.

**Mix** the cornstarch with the measured water in a small bowl until smooth. Stir in the remaining soy sauce.

**Heat** 1 tablespoon of the oil in a wok or large skillet over high heat. Add the bok choy and scallions and stir-fry for a couple of minutes, until the greens have wilted. Lift out onto a plate. Add the remaining oil to the pan, add the pork and sauté, turning once, for 3 minutes or until cooked through. Add the ginger, chile, and garlic and cook for another 1 minute.

**Return** the vegetables to the pan with the water chestnuts, noodles, and soy sauce mixture. Cook, stirring constantly, for 2–3 minutes, until hot and the sauce is thickened and glossy. Serve immediately.

**For easy pork & noodle soup**, prepare the pork and marinate it as above. Heat 1 tablespoon vegetable oil in a wok or saucepan and sauté the pork, turning the pieces during cooking, for 3 minutes, until golden. Add 3 cups pork or chicken stock, ¾-inch fresh ginger root, peeled and shredded, and a good pinch of dried red pepper flakes. Cover and cook gently for 15 minutes, until the pork is tender. Add 10 oz prepared fine noodles, 1⅓ cups frozen peas, 1 cup finely chopped fresh cilantro, 2 more tablespoons soy sauce, and 1 teaspoon rice vinegar. Heat gently for 2–3 minutes.

# braised beef with pickled walnuts

Serves **4**
Preparation time **20 minutes**
Cooking time **2½ hours**

2 tablespoons **all-purpose flour**
2 lb **chuck shoulder steak**, in one piece
2 tablespoons **olive oil**
2 **onions**, chopped
3 **celery sticks**, sliced
3 **bay leaves**
several **rosemary sprigs**
2 **garlic cloves**, crushed
2 cups **beef stock** (see page 108 for homemade)
1 chop chopped **walnuts**, lightly toasted
1 cup coarsely chopped drained **pickled walnuts** (available online)
2 tablespoons **whole-grain mustard**
⅓ cup **chopped parsley**, plus extra to garnish
**salt** and **black pepper**
**steamed green beans**, to serve

**Season** the flour with salt and black pepper on a plate. Coat the beef with the flour.

**Heat** the oil in a flameproof casserole and sauté the beef, in batches, until browned on all sides, turning it slowly in the oil. Transfer to a plate. Add the onions and celery to the casserole and sauté gently for 6–8 minutes, until softened.

**Tip** any flour leftover from coating into the casserole and cook, stirring, for 1 minute. Push the vegetables to one side and return the beef to the center of the pan. Add the bay leaves, rosemary, garlic, and stock. Bring to a simmer, stirring, then cover and cook in a preheated oven, at 300°F, for 1½ hours.

**Stir** all the walnuts, the mustard, and parsley into the casserole, replace the lid, and return to the oven for another 45 minutes. Season to taste with salt and black pepper, garnish with parsley and serve with steamed green beans.

**For braised liver with walnuts**, cut 1 lb liver into large pieces and coat in 2 teaspoons all-purpose flour seasoned with salt and black pepper. Melt 2 tablespoons butter with 2 tablespoons olive oil in a saucepan and sauté the liver briefly until lightly browned. Lift out with a slotted spoon onto a plate. Add 2 sliced onions to the pan and sauté until soft and browned. Return the liver to the pan with ⅔ cup chicken stock, 2 teaspoons whole-grain mustard, and ½ cup each chopped toasted walnuts and drained pickled walnuts. Heat through gently and season to taste with salt and black pepper before serving.

# sri lankan-style lamb curry

Serves **4**
Preparation time **10 minutes**
Cooking time about **35 minutes**

- 1 lb **boneless shoulder** or **leg of lamb**, diced
- 2 **red-skinned** or **white round potatoes**, peeled and cut into large chunks
- ¼ cup **olive oil**
- 1 (14½ oz) **can diced tomatoes**
- ⅔ cup **water**
- **salt** and **black pepper**

**Curry paste**

- 1 **onion**, grated
- 1 tablespoon peeled and finely chopped **fresh ginger root**
- 1 teaspoon finely chopped **garlic**
- ½ teaspoon **ground turmeric**
- 1 teaspoon **ground coriander**
- ½ teaspoon **ground cumin**
- ½ teaspoon **fennel seeds**
- ½ teaspoon **cumin seeds**
- 3 **cardamom pods**, crushed
- 2 **green chiles**, finely diced
- 2 inch **cinnamon stick**
- 2 **lemon grass stalks**, thinly sliced

**Make** the curry paste. Mix together all the ingredients in a large bowl. (For a milder curry, remove the seeds from the chiles before dicing.) Add the lamb and potatoes and mix well.

**Heat** the oil in a heavy saucepan or flameproof casserole, add the lamb-and-potato mixture, and cook, stirring, for 6–8 minutes.

**Stir** in the tomatoes and measured water and bring to a boil. Season well with salt and black pepper, then reduce the heat and simmer for 20–25 minutes, until the potatoes are cooked and the lamb is tender. Serve with toasted naans and Greek yogurt, if desired.

**For beef & potato curry**, use 1 lb top sirloin steak, cut into chunks, instead of the lamb. Cook the recipe as above and then serve with a generous sprinkling of chopped fresh cilantro.

# steak & kidney stew

Serves **4**
Preparation time **30 minutes**
Cooking time **2¼ hours**

1⅔ cups **all-purpose flour**, plus extra for dusting
1½ lb **chuck shoulder steak**, cut into chunks
5 oz **lamb kidneys**, cut into small pieces
3 tablespoons **vegetable oil**
2 **onions**, chopped
2½ cups **beef stock** (see page 108 for homemade)
½ teaspoon **baking powder**
½ cup **beef suet** or **lard**
about ⅔ cup **cold water**
1 (3 oz) **can smoked oysters**, drained and halved
3 tablespoons chopped **parsley**
3 tablespoons **Worcestershire sauce**
**beaten egg**, to glaze
**salt** and **black pepper**

**Season** 1½ tablespoons of the flour on a plate. Coat the beef and kidneys with the flour. Heat 2 tablespoons of the oil in a flameproof casserole and sauté the meat, in batches, until browned on all sides, lifting out with a slotted spoon onto a plate.

**Heat** the remaining oil in the casserole and sauté the onions for 5 minutes. Tip in any flour leftover from coating. Cook, stirring, for 1 minute. Blend in the stock.

**Return** all the meat to the casserole and bring to a simmer, stirring. Cover and cook in a preheated oven, at 325°F, for 1½ hours.

**Mix** together the remaining flour, baking powder, suet or lard, and a little salt and black pepper in a bowl. Add enough of the measured water, mixing with a blunt knife, to make a soft dough. Roll the dough out on a floured surface to a circle the same diameter as the casserole.

**Stir** the oysters, parsley, and Worcestershire sauce into the casserole and increase the oven temperature to 400°F. Lay the pastry dough over the filling and brush with beaten egg to glaze. Bake for about 25 minutes, until the pastry is pale golden.

**For steak & mushroom pie**, make the steak-and-kidney mixture as above, adding 2 cups quartered button mushrooms instead of the oysters. Once cooked, let cool. Roll out a sheet of ready-to-bake puff pastry, thawed if frozen, on a lightly floured surface until a little larger than the diameter of the casserole. Lay the pastry over the filling, pressing it against the dish. Brush with beaten egg and bake in a preheated oven, at 425°F, for 30 minutes or until risen and golden.

# pork saltado

serves **4**
preparation time **20 minutes**
cooking time **45 minutes**

3 **garlic cloves**, crushed
1 **red chile**, seeded and finely chopped
¼ cup **soy sauce**
1 ½ teaspoons lightly crushed **coriander seeds**
1 ½ teaspoons lightly crushed **cumin seeds**
1 tablespoon **white wine vinegar**
1 ½ lb **pork tenderloin**, cut into ¾ inch pieces
⅓ cup **vegetable oil**
6 **red-skinned** or **white round potatoes**, peeled and cut into ¾ inch pieces
4 **red onions**, sliced
4 **tomatoes**, skinned (see page 11) and coarsely chopped
¼ cup **water**
3 tablespoons chopped **fresh cilantro**
2 tablespoons chopped **mint**
**salt** and **black pepper**

**Mix** together the garlic, chile, soy sauce, coriander and cumin seeds, and vinegar in a small bowl and set aside.

**Season** the pork with salt and black pepper.

**Heat** 2 tablespoons of the oil in a large skillet and gently sauté the potatoes, stirring frequently, for about 15 minutes, until browned and tender. Lift out with a slotted spoon onto a plate.

**Add** another 2 tablespoons of the oil to the skillet and sauté the pork pieces, half at a time, for about 5 minutes, stirring frequently, until browned, lifting out with a slotted spoon onto the plate. Heat the remaining oil in the skillet and gently sauté the onions for about 10 minutes, until softened and browned. Add the tomatoes, garlic mixture, and measured water and mix.

**Return** the pork and potatoes to the skillet and cook gently for 10 minutes, until the pork is cooked through and tender and the tomatoes are pulpy. Stir in the chopped cilantro and mint and check the seasoning, adding a little salt and black pepper, if necessary.

**For crispy-cooked kale**, to serve as a side dish, wash 3 cups shredded curly kale and pat dry with paper towels. Place in a bowl and drizzle with 1 tablespoon vegetable oil. Sprinkle with 1 teaspoon granulated sugar and season with salt and black pepper. Mix the ingredients together thoroughly. (This is best done with your hands.) Turn into an oiled roasting pan and cook in a preheated oven, at 375°F, for 10 minutes, until crispy, turning the kale halfway through cooking.

# beef goulash

Serves **8**
Preparation time **10 minutes**
Cooking time **2–2½ hours**

3 lb **chuck shoulder steak**
¼ cup **olive oil**
2 **onions**, sliced
2 **red bell peppers**, cored, seeded, and diced
1 tablespoon **smoked paprika**
2 tablespoons chopped **marjoram**
1 teaspoon **caraway seeds**
4 cups **beef stock** (see below for homemade)
⅓ cup **tomato paste**
**salt** and **black pepper**
**French bread**, to serve

**Cut** the steak into large chunks. Heat the oil in a flameproof casserole and sauté the steak, in batches, until browned on all sides, lifting out with a slotted spoon onto a plate.

**Add** the onions and red bell peppers to the casserole and cook gently for 10 minutes, until softened. Stir in the paprika, marjoram, and caraway seeds and cook, stirring, for 1 minute.

**Return** the steak to the casserole, add the stock, tomato paste, and salt and black pepper to taste, and bring to a boil, stirring. Reduce the heat, cover, and cook gently for 1½–2 hours. If the sauce needs thickening, uncover for the final 30 minutes. Serve with French bread.

**For homemade beef stock**, put 1½ lb shin of beef, cut into chunks, in a large saucepan and add 2 chopped onions, 2–3 chopped carrots, 2 coarsely chopped celery sticks, 1 bay leaf, 1 bouquet garni, 4–6 black peppercorns, and 7½ cups cold water. Slowly bring to a boil, then reduce the heat, cover with a well-fitting lid, and simmer gently for 2 hours, skimming off any scum that rises to the surface. Strain through a fine strainer, discarding the solids, and let cool. Cover and store in the refrigerator for up to several days or freeze for up to 6 months. This makes about 7 cups.

# lamb with great Northern beans

Serves **4**
Preparation time **25 minutes**, plus overnight soaking
Cooking time **1½–1¾ hours**

1⅓ cups **dried great Northern beans**
½ **boneless leg of lamb** in one piece, about 1¾ lb
¼ cup **olive oil**
3 cups halved **cherry tomatoes**
1 teaspoon **granulated sugar**
2 **red onions**, chopped
8 **garlic cloves**, peeled and left whole
2 cups **lamb stock** (see below for homemade)
1 tablespoon chopped **rosemary**
3 tablespoons **tomato paste**
2 tablespoons **capers in brine**, rinsed and drained
**salt** and **black pepper**

**Soak** the beans in a bowl of cold water overnight. Drain and transfer to a flameproof casserole. Cover with fresh cold water, bring to a boil, and cook for 15 minutes. Drain and set aside. Discard any areas of excess fat from the lamb and cut the meat into 8 large chunky pieces. Season with salt and black pepper and set aside.

**Wipe** out the casserole. Heat 3 tablespoons of the oil and sauté the lamb, in two batches, until browned on all sides, lifting out with a slotted spoon onto a plate. Add the tomatoes and sugar to the casserole and sauté, turning in the oil, for 3 minutes. Slide out onto a plate and wipe out the pan. Add the remaining oil and onions and sauté for 5 minutes. Add the beans, garlic, stock, rosemary, and tomato paste. Bring to a boil, then reduce the heat, cover, and cook for 45 minutes or until the beans are tender. The water should be almost absorbed; if not, uncover, increase the heat, and reduce.

**Stir** in the capers and push the lamb down into the beans. Replace the lid and cook gently for 8–10 minutes so the lamb is still pink in the center. (For well-cooked, cook an extra 15 minutes.) Stir in the tomatoes and heat. Season to taste and let stand for 15 minutes.

**For homemade lamb stock**, heat 1 tablespoon olive oil in a large saucepan and sauté 1 lb lamb bones until browned all over. Drain off the fat and add 1 large chopped onion, 2 chopped carrots, 2 chopped celery sticks, 2 bay leaves, several thyme sprigs, and 1 teaspoon peppercorns. Cover with water and bring to a boil. Reduce the heat and cook for 2½–3 hours. Strain through a strainer and let cool. Cover and store in the refrigerator for up to several days or freeze.

# jamaican goat curry

Serves **4**
Preparation time **25 minutes**, plus marinating
Cooking time about **2½ hours**

- 1½ inch piece **fresh ginger root**, peeled and grated
- 1 **Scotch bonnet chile,** seeded and finely chopped
- 2 teaspoons **ground cumin**
- 2 teaspoons **ground coriander**
- ½ teaspoon **ground allspice**
- ½ teaspoon **ground turmeric**
- 1½ lb **boneless shoulder of goat**, cut into small cubes
- 2 tablespoons **vegetable oil**
- 2 **onions**, chopped
- 3 **garlic cloves**, crushed
- 1 cup **lamb** or **chicken stock** (see pages 110 and 36 for homemade)
- 1¾ cups **canned coconut milk**
- 4 **tomatoes**, skinned (see page 11) and coarsely chopped
- 4 **Yukon gold** or **white round potatoes,** peeled and cut into ¾ inch dice
- **salt** and **black pepper**

**Mix** together the ginger, chile, and ground spices. Put the goat in a nonmetallic bowl, add the spice blend, and mix together well. Cover loosely and let marinate in the refrigerator for several hours or overnight.

**Heat** the oil in a flameproof casserole and sauté the goat, in batches, until deep golden on all sides, lifting out with a slotted spoon onto a plate. Add the onions to the casserole and sauté gently for 5 minutes.

**Stir** in the garlic, stock, coconut milk, and tomatoes and bring to a simmer. Return the goat to the casserole, cover, and cook in a preheated oven, at 300°F, for 1½ hours or until the goat is tender. Add the potatoes to the casserole and return to the oven for another 30–40 minutes, until tender. Season to taste and serve in bowls.

**For Caribbean rice**, to serve as an accompaniment, heat 2 tablespoons vegetable oil in a large saucepan with a tight-fitting lid and sauté 1 small chopped onion for 5 minutes, until soft. Add 2 crushed garlic cloves, 1 teaspoon chopped thyme, and ¼ teaspoon ground allspice. Rinse and drain 1½ cups long-grain white rice. Add to the pan and cook, stirring, for 1 minute. Pour in 1¾ cups canned coconut milk and 1 cup vegetable or chicken stock. Bring to a boil, then reduce the heat to its lowest setting and add a Scotch bonnet chile. Cover and cook gently, stirring once or twice, for about 12 minutes, until the rice is just tender and the liquid has been absorbed. Stir in 1 (15 oz) can red kidney beans or cranberry beans, rinsed and drained, and 2 finely chopped scallions. Remove the chile, heat through, and season to taste.

# beef & potato hash

Serves **4**
Preparation time **15 minutes**
Cooking time **50 minutes**

2 tablespoons **vegetable oil**
1 1/2 lb **ground beef**
1 **fennel bulb**, trimmed and chopped
2 **celery sticks**, chopped
2 teaspoons **cornstarch**
2 cups **beef stock** (see page 108 for homemade)
3 tablespoons **tomato paste**
6 **red-skinned** or **white round potatoes**, peeled and cut into 3/4 inch chunks
4 **star anise**, broken into pieces and crushed using a mortar and pestle
3 tablespoons **soy sauce**
1 tablespoon packed **light brown sugar**
1/3 cup coarsely chopped **fresh cilantro**
**salt** and **black pepper**

**Heat** 1 tablespoon of the vegetable oil in a large, heavy skillet and sauté the ground beef for 10 minutes, breaking it up with a wooden spoon and stirring until browned and all the moisture has evaporated.

**Push** the meat to one side of the skillet, add the remaining oil, fennel, and celery, and sauté for 5 minutes, until softened. Mix the cornstarch with a little of the stock in a small bowl until smooth. Add to the skillet with the remaining stock, tomato paste, potatoes, and star anise.

**Bring** to a simmer, stirring, then reduce the heat and cover with a lid or aluminum foil. Cook gently for about 30 minutes, until the potatoes are tender, stirring occasionally and adding a dash more water if the dish starts to dry out.

**Stir** in the soy sauce and sugar and cook for another 5 minutes, uncovered, if necessary, to thicken the juices. Season to taste with salt and black pepper and stir in the cilantro before serving.

**For watercress salad**, to serve as an accompaniment, remove any tough stems from 2 bunches of watercress. Peel 1/2 cucumber and cut in half lengthwise. Scoop out the seeds and thinly slice the flesh. Add to the watercress in a salad bowl and sprinkle with 1/2 bunch of scallions, finely chopped. Whisk 3 tablespoons peanut or vegetable oil with 2 teaspoons rice vinegar, 1/2 teaspoon granulated sugar, and a little salt and black pepper. Drizzle the dressing over the salad.

# indian lamb curry

Serves **4**
Preparation time **15 minutes**
Cooking time **1¾ hours**

⅓ cup **blanched almonds**, coarsely chopped
3 tablespoons **butter** or **ghee** (clarified butter)
**8 cloves**
½ teaspoon **dried red pepper flakes**
10 **cardamom pods**
1 tablespoon lightly crushed **cumin seeds**
1 tablespoon lightly crushed **coriander seeds**
1½ inch piece **fresh ginger root**, grated
½ teaspoon **ground turmeric**
2 **onions**, chopped
3 **garlic cloves**, coarsely chopped
2 lb **boneless shoulder of lamb**, cut into small chunks
6 **tomatoes**, skinned (see page 11) and coarsely chopped
½ cup **plain yogurt**
**salt** and **black pepper**
**chopped cilantro**, to garnish

**Heat** a dry flameproof casserole, add the almonds, and cook for 1 minute, until toasted.

**Melt** the butter or ghee in the casserole and add the cloves, red pepper flakes, cardamom, cumin, coriander, ginge, and turmeric. Sauté over gentle heat for 3 minutes. Add the onions and sauté for 5 minutes, stirring constantly, until they begin to brown. Add the garlic for the last few minutes.

**Transfer** the contents of the casserole to a food processor, add ½ cup cold water, and process to a smooth paste, scraping down the mixture from the side of the bowl.

**Return** the paste to the casserole and stir in the lamb, tomatoes, and ½ cup cold water. Bring to a simmer, then reduce the heat to its lowest setting. Stir in the yogurt. Cook gently, uncovered and stirring the mixture occasionally, for about 1½ hours or until the lamb is tender and the juices thickened. Season and then garnish with cilantro to serve.

**For pilaf rice**, to serve as a side dish, rinse and drain 1¾ cups basmati rice. Melt 2 tablespoons butter in a saucepan with a tight-fitting lid and gently sauté 2 finely chopped shallots with 1 teaspoon cardamom pods and 2 tablespoons black or yellow mustard seeds. When the seeds start to pop, stir in the rice and cook, stirring, for 1 minute. Add 2 cups vegetable or chicken stock and ¼ teaspoon ground turmeric. Bring to a boil, reduce the heat to its lowest setting, cover, and cook for 12–15 minutes, until the rice is tender and the water has been absorbed. Fluff up the rice with a fork and season to taste before serving.

# pork with maple-roasted roots

Serves **6**
Preparation time **30 minutes**
Cooking time about **5 hours**

2 tablesppons chopped **thyme leaves**
5 **garlic cloves**, crushed
½ teaspoon **caraway seeds**
1 teaspoon **celery salt**
5½ lb **boneless shoulder of pork**, skin scored
10 oz **pearl onions** or **shallots**
2½ lb **new potatoes**, scrubbed
4 **parsnips,** cut into wedges
6 **carrots**, cut into wedges
½ cup **maple syrup**
⅔ cup **dry white wine**
1¼ cups **beef** or **chicken stock** (see page 108 or 36 for homemade)
**salt** and **black pepper**

**Mix** together the thyme, garlic, celery salt, and black pepper. Use a sharp knife to cut several deep slits through the pork skin into the meat. Pack the garlic mixture into the slits. Rub salt over the skin. Place the pork in a large roasting pan and roast in a preheated oven, at 425°F, for 30 minutes. Reduce the oven temperature to 275°F and roast for another 2 hours. Put the onions or shallots in a heatproof bowl, cover with boiling water, and let stand. Drain and rinse in cold water. Peel away the skins, leaving the onions or shallots whole. Add to the pan with the vegetables, turning in the fat. Return to the oven for 2 hours, turning occasionally.

**Transfer** the pork to a carving plate. Cover with a sheet of aluminum foil and let rest in a warm place. Increase the oven temperature to at 425°F. Drain off the excess fat from the pan and brush the vegetables with the maple syrup. Return to the oven for 25–30 minutes, turning once, until golden. Lift out into a dish.

**Skim** off the fat in the pan, retaining the meaty juices. Add the wine and stock, bring to a boil on the stove, and cook for about 5 minutes, until slightly thickened. Serve the carved meat with the vegetables and gravy.

**For apple & pear butter**, to serve alongside, place 2 each peeled, cored, and chopped apples and pears in a saucepan with 1 tablespoon granulated sugar, 1 tablespoon water, and a pinch of ground cloves. Cook, stirring, for 10–15 minutes, until tender. Mash with a potato masher. Cook a little longer to thicken. Add 4 tablespoons unsalted butter, diced, a squeeze of lemon juice, and stir until melted. Turn into a serving dish and let cool. Cover and chill.

# beef rendang

Serves **4**
Preparation time **25 minutes**
Cooking time **3 hours**

2 **lemon grass stalks**
6 **kaffir lime leaves**
1 large **onion**, coarsely chopped
4 **garlic cloves**, crushed
1 1/4 inch piece of **fresh ginger root**, peeled and coarsely chopped
1 1/2 teaspoons **ground coriander**
1/2 teaspoon dried **red pepper flakes**
1/2 teaspoon **salt**
1/2 teaspoon **ground turmeric**
4 tablespoons **water**
2 tablespoons **vegetable oil**
1 3/4 lb **shin of beef**, cut into large chunks
1 3/4 cups **canned coconut milk**
1 tablespoon packed **palm sugar** or **light brown sugar**
**chopped parsley**, to garnish

**Discard** the woody ends of the lemon grass and coarsely chop. Put into a food processor with the lime leaves, onion, garlic, ginger, coriander, red pepper flakes, salt, turmeric, and measured water. Process to a smooth paste, scraping down the mixture from the side of the bowl.

**Heat** the oil in a flameproof casserole and sauté the beef, in batches, until browned on all sides, lifting out with a slotted spoon onto a plate. Tip in the spice paste and cook over gentle heat, stirring, for 4–5 minutes or until most of the moisture has evaporated. (Add a dash of water if the paste starts to stick to the pan.)

**Stir** the coconut milk and sugar into the casserole and bring to a simmer. Return the beef to the pan, cover, and cook in a preheated oven, at 300°F, for about 2 1/2 hours or until the meat is tender.

**Remove** the lid and return the casserole to the stove. Cook, stirring, for 8–10 minutes, until the moisture has evaporated and the sauce thickly coats the meat. Sprinkle with the chopped parsley and serve.

**For spiced jasmine rice**, to serve as accompaniment, rinse and drain 1 1/2 cups jasmine or other long-grain rice. Heat 2 tablespoons vegetable oil in a saucepan with a tight-fitting lid and sauté 1 halved cinnamon stick, 10 crushed cardamom pods, and 1 teaspoon crushed coriander seeds for 1 minute. Add the rice and cook, stirring, for 2 minutes. Pour in 2 cups water and bring to a boil. Reduce the heat to its lowest setting, cover, and cook for 12–15 minutes, or as the package directions, until tender and the water absorbed. Fluff up with a fork, stir in 1/4 cup chopped cilantro and a little salt, and serve.

# braised lamb shanks & tapenade

Serves **4**
Preparation time **15 minutes**
Cooking time **2¼ hours**

1 tablespoon **all-purpose flour**
4 large **lamb shanks**
2 tablespoons **olive oil**
1 large **onion**, chopped
⅔ cup **dry white wine**
1¼ cups **lamb** or **chicken stock** (see pages 110 and 36 for homemade)
finely grated rind of **1 small orange**
⅔ cup store-bought or homemade **black olive tapenade** (see below)
½ (14 oz) can **artichoke hearts** in oil, drained and sliced
**salt** and **black pepper**
**basil leaves**, to garnish
**ciabatta**, to serve

**Season** the flour with salt and black pepper on a plate. Coat the lamb shanks with the flour.

**Heat** the oil in a large flameproof casserole and sauté the lamb shanks for 5 minutes, until browned on all sides, then transfer the lamb to a plate. Add the onion to the casserole and sauté for 5 minutes, until softened.

**Stir** the wine and stock into the casserole and bring to a gentle simmer. Add the orange rind and return the lamb to the pan. Cover and cook in a preheated oven, at 325°F, for 1½ hours.

**Spoon** the tapenade around the lamb, stirring it into the cooking juices. Return the casserole to the oven for another 30 minutes or until the lamb is tender and can be pulled easily from the bone with a fork.

**Transfer** the casserole to the stove and cook gently, uncovered, to thicken the sauce if thin. Season to taste with salt and black pepper and sprinkle the artichokes around the shanks. Cook for 5 minutes to heat through. Sprinkle with basil leaves and serve with ciabatta.

**For homemade tapenade**, put 1 cup pitted black ripe olives, 2 tablespoons rinsed and drained capers in brine, 2 chopped garlic cloves, 1 cup chopped sun-dried tomatoes, 6 drained canned anchovy fillets, and ¼ cup parsley in a food processor. Process until smooth, scraping down the mixture from the side of the bowl. Add ½ cup olive oil and process again until smooth. Season with a little black pepper and transfer to a bowl. Cover and refrigerate for up to a week.

# chorizo & chickpea stew

Serves **4**
Preparation time **5 minutes**
Cooking time **25 minutes**

1 lb **new potatoes**, scrubbed
1 teaspoon **olive oil**
2 **red onions**, chopped
2 **red bell peppers**, cored, seeded, and chopped
4 oz **chorizo sausage**, thinly sliced
8 **plum tomatoes**, chopped, or 1 (14½ oz) **can diced tomatoes**, drained
1 (15 oz) **can chickpeas**, rinsed and drained
2 tablespoons chopped **parsley**, to garnish
**garlic bread**, to serve

**Cook** the potatoes in a saucepan of boiling water for 12–15 minutes, until tender. Drain and then slice.

**Meanwhile,** heat the oil in a large skillet and sauté the onions and red bell peppers over medium heat for 3–4 minutes. Add the chorizo and cook, turning frequently, for 2 minutes.

**Stir** the potato slices, tomatoes, and chickpeas into the skillet and bring to a boil. Reduce the heat and cook gently for 10 minutes.

**Sprinkle** with the parsley to garnish and serve with some hot garlic bread to mop up all the juices.

**For sausage & mixed bean stew**, cook the potatoes, then sauté the onions and red bell peppers in the oil as above. Add 4 pork link sausages instead of the chorizo to the skillet and cook for 4–5 minutes, until browned on all sides. Lift the sausages from the skillet and cut each into 6 thick slices. Return to the skillet and add the potato slices and tomatoes as above, but replace the chickpeas with 2 cups rinsed and drained canned mixed beans, such as kidney beans, pinto beans, and chickpeas. Bring to a boil and cook as above. If you prefer a slightly hotter stew, add 1 seeded and chopped red chile when sautéing the onions and bell peppers.

# pot-roasted lamb with figs

Serves **6**
Preparation time **30 minutes**, plus resting
Cooking time **2¼ hours**

- ⅔ cup chopped **pistachio nuts**, and toasted
- ½ cup chopped **dried figs**
- ¼ teaspoon **ground cloves**
- 3 tablespoons **chopped mint**
- 1 teaspoon **rose water**
- 3 lb **boneless rolled shoulder of lamb**
- 2 tablespoons **honey**
- 1 cup **dry white wine**
- 1½ lb **new potatoes,** scrubbed
- 3 tablespoons **olive oil**
- 4 **small zucchini**, cut into thick slices
- **salt** and **black pepper**

**Mix** together the pistachio nuts, figs, cloves, mint, rose water, and a little salt and black pepper in a bowl.

**Unroll** the lamb, removing the string, and pack the stuffing down the center and into the cavities and folds of the lamb. Reroll and secure with more string. Sit in a large roasting pan, fat side up, and rub a little salt and black pepper over the surface. Roast in a preheated oven, at 425°F, for 30 minutes.

**Reduce** the oven temperature to at 350°F. Brush the honey over the lamb, then pour the wine into the roasting pan. Brush the potatoes with the oil, then sprinkle into the pan. Season to taste with salt and black pepper. Return to the oven for another 1¼ hours.

**Add** the zucchini to the roasting pan, turning them in the juices, and return to the oven for 30 minutes. Let rest in a warm place for 20 minutes before carving the lamb.

**For apricot, cinnamon & walnut stuffing**, to use instead of the pistachio stuffing, heat 1 tablespoon vegetable oil in a skillet and gently sauté 1 chopped onion until softened. Transfer to a bowl and add ⅔ cup chopped walnuts, ¾ cup chopped dried apricots, the finely grated rind of 2 lemons, and ½ teaspoon ground cinnamon. Mix well and finish the recipe as above.

# chestnut, rice & pancetta soup

Serves **4**
Preparation time **10 minutes**
Cooking time **35 minutes**

4 tablespoons **butter**
5 oz **pancetta**, diced
1 **onion,** finely chopped
2 cups **cooked, peeled chestnuts**
¾ cup **risotto rice**
2 cups **chicken stock** (see page 36 for homemade)
⅔ cup **milk**
**salt** and **black pepper**

**Melt** half the butter in a saucepan and cook the pancetta and onion over medium heat for 10 minutes.

**Cut** the chestnuts in half and add to the pan with the rice and stock. Bring to a boil, then reduce the heat and cook gently for 20 minutes or until the rice is tender and most of the liquid has been absorbed.

**Heat** the milk in a small saucepan until lukewrm, then stir into the rice with the remaining butter. Season to taste with salt and black pepper. Cover and let stand for about 5 minutes before serving.

**For fennel, rice & pancetta soup with garlic & anchovies**, cook the pancetta in 2 tablespoons butter as above with 1 large trimmed and thinly sliced fennel bulb instead of the onion. Then add the rice and stock to the pan, omitting the chestnuts, and cook as above until the rice is tender. Meanwhile, put ¼ cup milk, 6 peeled whole garlic cloves, and 2½ (2 oz) cans drained anchovy fillets in a small saucepan and cook gently for 15 minutes, without letting the milk boil, until the anchovies have melted into the milk and the garlic is soft. Use the back of a fork to mash the garlic against the side of the pan, then add 6 tablespoons butter and ⅓ cup extra virgin olive oil and stir until the butter has melted. Stir this mixture into the soup in place of the milk, then season to taste with salt and black pepper, cover, and let stand for 5 minutes before serving.

# sausage ragu with polenta crust

Serves **4**
Preparation time **15 minutes**
Cooking time **1 hour**

1½ lb **pork link sausages with garlic or herbs**
¼ cup **olive oil**
2 **onions**, chopped
2 **garlic cloves**, crushed
1½ teaspoons **fennel seeds**
1½ cups **tomato puree** or **tomato sauce**
⅔ cup **red wine**
¼ cup **tomato paste**
2 tablespoons chopped **oregano**
1 (18-ounce) **polenta log** or 1-quantity homemade **polenta** (see below)
1 cup freshly grated **Parmesan cheese**
½ cup shredded **sharp cheddar cheese**
**salt** and **black pepper**

**Split** the casings of the sausages with a knife, peel away, and discard the casings.

**Heat** the oil in a shallow, flameproof casserole or heavy skillet and gently sauté the onions for 10 minutes, until softened and pale golden, adding the garlic for the last couple of minutes. Add the sausages and fennel seeds and cook for 10 minutes, breaking up the sausages with a wooden spoon, until golden.

**Stir** in the tomato puree or tomato sauce, wine, tomato paste, and oregano. Bring to a simmer, then reduce the heat to its lowest setting, cover, and cook gently for 30 minutes, until the sauce is thick and pulpy. Season to taste with salt and black pepper.

**Break** up the polenta into small pieces and crumble it over the sausages. Sprinkle with the Parmesan and cheddar and cook under a preheated moderate broiler for about 5 minutes, until the cheese is melting and the polenta is heated through.

**For homemade polenta**, bring 3¾ cups water to a boil with 1 teaspoon salt in a saucepan. Add 1 cup instant polenta in a stream, whisking constantly to prevent lumps from forming. Once it starts to thicken, use a wooden spoon to stir the polenta while it cooks for about 5 minutes, until thick and beginning to hold its shape. Line a baking sheet with parchment paper and pour out the polenta onto it. Let stand until cold, then use as above.

# pork shins "osso bucco"

Serves **4–5**
Preparation time **15 minutes**
Cooking time **2–2½ hours**

1 tablespoon **all-purpose flour**
2 lb **shin of pork**, thickly sliced
3 tablespoons **olive oil**
2 **onions**, finely chopped
2 **carrots**, diced
2 **celery sticks**, thinly sliced
1¼ cups **dry white wine**
1 (14½ oz) **can plum tomatoes**
¼ cup **tomato paste**
⅔ cup **chicken stock** (see page 36 for homemade)
1 **garlic clove**, finely chopped
finely grated rind of 1 **lemon**
3 tablespoons chopped **parsley**
**salt** and **black pepper**

**Season** the flour with salt and black pepper on a plate. Coat the pork with the flour.

**Heat** 2 tablespoons of the oil in a large flameproof casserole and sauté the pork, in batches, until browned on both sides, lifting out with a slotted spoon onto a plate. Add the remaining oil to the casserole and gently sauté the onions, carrots, and celery for 10 minutes, until softened. Add any flour leftover from coating and cook, stirring, for 1 minute.

**Blend** in the wine and bring to a boil, stirring. Stir in the tomatoes, tomato paste, stock, and a little salt and black pepper. Return the pork to the casserole, cover, and cook in a preheated oven, at 325°F, for 1½–2 hours, until the meat is tender.

**Mix** together the garlic, lemon rind, and parsley, sprinkle the mixture over the casserole, and serve.

**For risotto Milanese**, to serve as an accompaniment, melt 2 tablespoons butter in a large saucepan and gently sauté 1 finely chopped onion for 5 minutes, until softened. Add 1½ cups risotto rice and cook, stirring, for 2 minutes. Gradually add 15 cups hot chicken stock to the pan, a ladleful at a time, cooking and stirring until each ladleful has been absorbed before adding the next. This should take 20–25 minutes, by which time the rice should be tender but retaining a little bite and the consistency creamy. You may not need all the stock. Crumble in 1 teaspoon saffron threads toward the end of cooking. Once cooked, beat in another 2 tablespoons butter and ½ cup freshly grated Parmesan cheese.

# molasses & mustard beans

Serves **6**
Preparation time **10 minutes**
Cooking time **1 hour 35 minutes**

1 **carrot**, diced
1 **celery stick**, chopped
1 **onion**, chopped
2 **garlic cloves**, crushed
2 (15 oz) cans **soybeans**, drained, or 2¾ cups frozen shelled edamame, thawed
2¾ cups **tomato puree** or **tomato sauce**
3 oz **smoked bacon slices**, diced
2 tablespoons **molasses**
2 teaspoons **Dijon mustard**
**salt** and **black pepper**

**Place** all the ingredients in a flameproof casserole and bring slowly to a boil, stirring occasionally.

**Cover** and bake in a preheated oven, at 325°F, for 1 hour.

**Remove** the lid and bake for another 30 minutes. Serve at once.

**For garlic-rubbed sourdough bread**, to serve as an accompaniment, heat a ridged grill pan or large, dry skillet until hot and cook 6 thick slices of sourdough bread for 2 minutes on each side, until lightly charred. Rub each bread slice with the cut sides of 1–2 peeled and halved garlic cloves and drizzle with extra virgin olive oil.

# fish & seafood

# crab & coconut chowder

Serves **4**
Preparation time **15 minutes**
Cooking time **50 minutes**

2 tablespoons **butter**
1 tablespoon **vegetable oil**
1 large **onion**, chopped
8 oz **lean belly pork**, finely diced
2 **garlic cloves**, crushed
⅔ cup **dry white wine**
¾ cup **canned diced tomatoes**
1¾ cups **coconut milk**
1 teaspoon **medium curry paste**
3 **red-skinned** or **white round potatoes**, peeled and diced
10 oz **white** and **brown crabmeat**
3 tablespoons **heavy cream**
**salt** and **black pepper**
**crusty bread**, to serve

**Melt** the butter with the oil in a large saucepan and gently sauté the onion and pork, stirring, for about 10 minutes, until lightly browned. Stir in the garlic and sauté for 1 minute. Lift the pork out with a slotted spoon onto a plate.

**Add** the wine to the pan, bring to a boil, and boil for about 5 minutes, until slightly reduced.

**Return** the pork to the pan, add the tomatoes, coconut milk, curry paste, and potatoes and heat until simmering. Reduce the heat to its lowest setting, cover, and cook for 30 minutes.

**Stir** in the crabmeat and cream, heat through thoroughly, and season to taste with salt and black pepper. Serve hot with crusty bread, if liked.

**For smoked haddock & corn chowder,** melt 2 tablespoons butter in a large saucepan and gently sauté 1 chopped onion and 1 chopped celery stick. Stir in 2 teaspoons crushed coriander seeds, ¼ teaspoon ground turmeric, 2½ cups milk, and 2 cups fish or chicken stock. Bring just to a boil, then reduce the heat to its lowest setting. Stir in 4 diced, peeled red-skinned or white round potatoes and 1¼ lb diced skinless smoked haddock fillet. Cover and cook gently for 10 minutes, then stir in 1⅓ cups corn kernels and cook for another 10 minutes. Season to taste with black pepper and serve.

# braised pollock with lentils

Serves **4**
Preparation time **15 minutes**
Cooking time **50 minutes**

¼ cup **olive oil**
1 **onion**, finely chopped
4 **garlic cloves**, crushed
2 teaspoons finely chopped **rosemary, savory**, or **thyme**
1 (15 oz) **can green lentils** or 2 cups **cooked lentils**
1 (14½ oz) **can diced tomatoes**
2 teaspoons **granulated sugar**
⅔ cup **fish stock** (see page 178 for homemade)
1¼ lb **skinless Alaskan pollock fillets**
¼ cup chopped **parsley**
1 (2 oz) **can anchovy fillets**, drained and chopped
**salt** and **black pepper**
**garlic mayonnaise**, to serve

**Heat** 2 tablespoons of the oil in a flameproof casserole and gently sauté the onion for 6–8 minutes, until lightly browned. Add the garlic and herb and cook for about 2 minutes.

**Drain** the lentils and stir into the casserole with the tomatoes, sugar, and stock. Bring to a simmer, then cover and cook in a preheated oven, at 350°F, for 10 minutes.

**Meanwhile,** check over the fish for any stray bones and cut into 8 pieces. Season with salt and black pepper.

**Stir** the parsley and anchovies into the casserole. Nestle the fish down into the lentils and drizzle the remaining oil over the fish. Replace the lid and return to the oven for another 25 minutes or until the fish is cooked through. Serve with spoonfuls of garlic mayonnaise.

**For salsa verde sauce**, to serve as an alternative accompaniment to the garlic mayonnaise, put ¼ cup coarsely chopped parsley and ⅓ cup coarsely chopped basil in a food processor with 1 coarsely chopped garlic clove, 4 pitted green olives, 1 tablespoon rinsed and drained capers in brine, and ½ teaspoon Dijon mustard. Process until finely chopped. Add 1 tablespoon lemon juice and ½ cup olive oil and process to make a thick sauce. Season to taste with salt and black pepper, adding a dash more lemon juice, if desired, for extra tang.

# mediterranean fish stew

Serves **4–6**
Preparation time **30 minutes**
Cooking time **45 minutes**

1 large handful of **fresh mussels**
1 ½ lb mixed **skinless white fish fillets,** such as Alaskan pollock, cod, halibut, or red snapper
¼ cup **olive oil**
1 large **onion**, chopped
2 small **fennel bulbs**, trimmed and chopped
5 **garlic cloves**, crushed
3 pared strips of **orange rind**
2 (14½ oz) **cans diced tomatoes**
2 teaspoons **granulated sugar**
¼ cup **tomato paste**
2 cups **fish stock** (see page 178 for homemade)
1 teaspoon **saffron threads**
8 oz cleaned **squid tubes**, cut into rings
**salt** and **black pepper**

**Scrub** the mussels. Scrape off any barnacles and pull away any beards. Discard those that are damaged or open and do not close when tapped firmly. Check over the fish for any stray bones and cut into chunky pieces. Season with salt and black pepper.

**Heat** the oil in a large flameproof casserole and sauté the onion for 5 minutes. Add the fennel and sauté, stirring, for 10 minutes. Add the garlic and orange rind and sauté for 2 minutes. Add the tomatoes, sugar, tomato paste, and fish stock. Crumble in the saffron and bring the stew to a gentle simmer. Cook gently, uncovered, for 15 minutes.

**Lower** the thickest, chunkiest pieces of fish into the stew. Reduce the heat to its lowest setting and cook for 5 minutes. Add the thin pieces of fish and the squid to the stew. Sprinkle the mussels on top and cover with a lid or aluminum foil. Cook for another 5 minutes or until the mussel shells have opened. Ladle into large bowls, discarding any mussel shells that remain closed.

**For homemade rouille**, to serve as a topping, spear a fork into a small red bell pepper and hold it over the stove on its highest setting until the skin blisters and browns. Remove from the heat and, when cool, peel off the skin. Coarsely chop the flesh, discarding the core and seeds. Place in a food processor or blender with 2 chopped garlic cloves, 1 seeded and chopped hot red chile, 1 egg yolk, and a little salt. Process to a paste. Add ½ cup fresh white bread crumbs and blend again until smooth. With the machine running, gradually drizzle in ½ cup olive oil in a thin stream. Season with salt, transfer to a serving dish, cover, and chill until ready. Serve spooned over the stew.

# mackerel with sesame noodles

Serves **2**
Preparation time **10 minutes**
Cooking time **12 minutes**

- 2 large **mackerel fillets**, about 4 oz each
- 2 tablespoons **teriyaki sauce**
- 2 teaspoons **sesame oil**
- 1 tablespoon **sesame seeds**
- ½ bunch of **scallions**, chopped
- 1 **garlic clove**, very thinly sliced
- 1 cup trimmed and diagonally sliced **green beans**
- 1¾ cups **fish stock** (see page 178 for homemade)
- 5 oz **medium prepared rice noodles**
- 1 teaspoon **granulated sugar**
- 2 teaspoons **lime juice**

**Cut** the mackerel into pieces and mix with the teriyaki sauce in a bowl.

**Warm** the sesame oil in a saucepan and add the sesame seeds, scallions, garlic, and green beans. Heat through gently for 2 minutes.

**Add** the stock and bring to a gentle simmer. Cover and cook for 5 minutes.

**Stir** the mackerel, noodles, sugar, and lime juice into the pan and cook gently for 2 minutes, until the mackerel is cooked and the broth is hot. Serve immediately.

**For quick pad thai**, mix ½ teaspoon cornstarch with 1 tablespoon lime juice in a small bowl until smooth. Add another 2 tablespoons lime juice, ½ teaspoon chili powder, 2 tablespoons granulated sugar, and 2 tablespoons Thai fish sauce. Heat 1 tablespoon vegetable oil in a large skillet or wok over high heat and stir-fry 5 oz peeled shrimp until they have turned pink. Add ½ bunch of scallions, chopped, 2 cups bean sprouts, ⅓ cup chopped salted peanuts, and 5 oz prepared rice noodles. Drizzle with the lime juice mixture and heat through, stirring, for a couple of minutes. Serve sprinkled with extra chopped peanuts and a small handful of chopped fresh cilantro.

# creamy garlic mussels

Serves **4**
Preparation time **15 minutes**
Cooking time **10 minutes**

3 lb **fresh mussels**
1 tablespoon **butter**
1 **onion**, finely chopped
6 **garlic cloves**, finely chopped
½ cup **white wine**
⅔ cup **light cream**
1 large handful of **flat leaf parsley**, coarsely chopped
**salt** and **black pepper**
**crusty bread**, to serve

**Scrub** the mussels in cold water. Scrape off any barnacles and pull away the dark hairy beards. Discard any with damaged shells or open ones that do not close when tapped firmly with a knife.

**Melt** the butter in a large saucepan and gently sauté the onion and garlic for 2–3 minutes, until transparent and softened.

**Increase** the heat and put the mussels into the pan with the wine. Cover and cook, shaking the pan frequently, for 4–5 minutes, until all the shells have opened. Discard any that remain closed.

**Pour** in the cream and heat through briefly, stirring well. Add the parsley, season well with salt and black pepper, and serve immediately in large bowls, with crusty bread to mop up the juices.

**For mussels in spicy tomato sauce**, cook the onion and garlic as above in 1 tablespoon olive oil instead of the butter, together with 1 seeded and finely chopped red chile. Add 1 teaspoon paprika and cook, stirring, for 1 minute, then add 1 (14½ oz) can diced tomatoes. Season to taste with salt and black pepper, cover, and cook gently for 15 minutes. Meanwhile, scrub and debeard the mussels as above. Then stir the mussels into the tomato sauce and increase the heat. Cover and cook for 4–5 minutes, until all the shells have opened. Discard any that remain closed. Add the parsley and serve as above.

# spanish baked fish

Serves **4**
Preparation time **5 minutes**
Cooking time **25 minutes**

4 chunky **skinless hake**, **cod**, or **haddock fillets**, about 5 oz each
1/3 cup **extra virgin olive oil**
1/3 cup **pine nuts**
1/3 cup **raisins**
3 **garlic cloves**, thinly sliced
1 (10 oz) package **fresh spinach**, washed and drained
**lemon** or **lime wedges**, for squeezing over
**salt** and **black pepper**
**rustic bread**, to serve

**Season** the fish with salt and black pepper. Drizzle a little of the oil into a roasting pan. Add the fish, spacing the pieces slightly apart, and brush with the remaining oil. Sprinkle the pine nuts and raisins into the pan.

**Bake** in a preheated oven, at 375°F, for 20 minutes or until the fish is cooked through.

**Sprinkle** the garlic into the roasting pan. Pile the spinach on top of the fish, first making sure all the water has been thoroughly drained off the spinach. Season lightly with salt and black pepper and return to the oven for another 5 minutes, until the spinach has wilted.

**Pile** the spinach onto warm serving plates and lay the fish on top. Spoon the pine nuts, raisins, garlic, and cooking juices over the fish. Serve with lemon or lime wedges to squeeze over the fish and with warmed rustic bread.

**For quince alioli**, to serve as an accompaniment, put 3 tablespoons quince jelly in a bowl and beat with a small whisk to break the jelly up. Whisk in 1 crushed garlic clove, plenty of black pepper, and 2 teaspoons lemon or lime juice. Gradually whisk in 1/4 cup olive oil, a little at a time, until the consistency becomes smooth and thick. Transfer to a small bowl, cover, and chill until ready to serve.

# pea, dill & smoked salmon soup

Serves **4**
Preparation time **10 minutes**
Cooking time **30 minutes**

2 tablespoons **butter**
1 large **onion**, chopped
4 cups) **fish stock** (see page 178 for homemade)
1 lb **skinless lightly smoked salmon**
4 cups **fresh** or **frozen peas**
⅓ cup chopped **dill,** plus extra for sprinkling
3 tablespoons **crème fraîche** or **sour cream**, plus extra for topping
**salt** and **black pepper**

**Melt** the butter in a large saucepan and sauté the onion for 5 minutes, until softened. Add the stock and bring to a gentle simmer. Lower the fish into the pan and cook gently for 5 minutes, until the fish has turned opaque. Lift the fish out with a slotted spoon onto a plate.

**Add** the peas to the saucepan and bring to a boil. Reduce the heat to its lowest setting, cover, and cook for 15 minutes. Ladle about half the soup into a food processor or blender and process until smooth. Return to the pan.

**Flake** the salmon into small pieces and add to the pan with the dill and crème fraîche or sour cream. Heat through gently and season to taste with salt and black pepper.

**Ladle** the soup into serving bowls and spoon a little of the crème fraîche or sour cream on top of each. Serve sprinkled with extra dill.

**For creamed corn & cockle soup**, sauté the onion and add the stock as above. Add 3 cups frozen corn kernels and 3 peeled and diced red-skinned or white round potatoes. Reduce the heat to a gentle simmer and cook, covered, for 15 minutes. Add 8 oz cooked frozen cockles (not those preserved in vinegar) or small clams, 1 tablespoon tarragon leaves, and 1 teaspoon mild curry paste. Cook gently for another 5 minutes. Blend the soup, using an immersion blender or in a food processor, and stir in 3 tablespoons crème fraîche or sour cream. Reheat gently, season to taste with salt and black pepper, and serve.

# seafood casserole

Serves **4**
Preparation time **20 minutes**
Cooking time **15 minutes**

8 oz **fresh mussels**
8 oz **clams**
3 tablespoons **olive oil**
2 **red onions**, finely diced
2 **garlic cloves**, crushed
½ teaspoon **dried red pepper flakes**
8 oz **cleaned baby squid**, cut into thin strips, tentacles reserved
8 oz **raw shell-on jumbo shrimp**
⅔ cup **hot fish stock** (see page 178 for homemade)
⅔ cup **dry white wine**
½ teaspoon crumbled **saffron threads**
**8 tomatoes**, skinned (see page 11) and seeded
1 **bay leaf**
1 teaspoon **granulated sugar**
12 oz **red snapper** or **sea bass fillets**, cut into bite-size pieces
**salt** and **black pepper**

**Scrub** the mussels and clams in cold water. Scrape off any barnacles from the mussels and pull away the dark hairy beards. Discard any mussels or clams with damaged shells or open ones that do not close when tapped firmly with a knife. Set aside.

**Heat** the oil in a large saucepan and gently sauté the onions and garlic for 5 minutes. Stir in the red pepper flakes, then add the mussels and clams with the squid and shrimp and stir well.

**Stir** in the hot stock, wine, saffron, tomatoes, bay leaf, and sugar and season with salt and black pepper. Cover and cook for 5 minutes. Discard any mussels or clams that remain closed.

**Add** the fish, replace the lid, and cook gently for 5 minutes, until cooked through. Serve immediately.

**For creamy seafood stew**, replace the red onions with 2 white onions and cook with the garlic as above, adding 1 bunch of scallions, sliced, with the red pepper flakes. Add the seafood as above, stir in the stock, wine, saffron, bay leaf, and sugar, omitting the tomatoes, and bring to a boil. Season to taste with salt and black pepper and cook, uncovered, for about 5 minutes, until the wine has reduced by half. Stir in 1 cup crème fraîche and 1¼ cups heavy cream (or 2¼ cups heavy cream if you don't have crème fraîche) and cook for another 5 minutes. Mix 1 tablespoon cornstarch with 2 tablespoons cold water in a cup until smooth and add to the casserole with 2 tablespoons chopped parsley and the finely grated rind of 1 lemon. Cook, stirring, until slightly thickened. Serve with rice and a simple salad.

# smoked fish pie

Serves **4**
Preparation time **35 minutes**, plus chilling
Cooking time **1 hour**

1 1/4 lb **skinless smoked haddock, Alaskan pollock**, or **cod fillets**
1 teaspoon **cornstarch**
4 **eggs**, soft-boiled shelled
1 **bunch of scallions**, chopped
1 tablespoon **green peppercorns**, rinsed and drained
1/4 cup chopped **parsley**
1 cup **fresh shelled peas**
2 cups store-bought or homemade **cheese sauce** (see below)

**Potato pastry dough**
2 **russet potatoes**
2 cups **all-purpose flour**, plus extra for dusting
1/2 teaspoon **sea salt flakes**, plus extra for sprinkling
6 tablespoons **firm butter**, cut into small pieces
1/4 cup **firm lard**, diced
1 teaspoon **Dijon mustard**
**beaten egg**, to glaze

**Make** the potato pastry dough. Finely grate the potatoes, then pat dry between several layers of paper towels. Place the flour in a bowl, add the salt, butter, and lard, and rub in with the fingertips until the mixture resembles coarse bread crumbs. Mix in the potatoes. Mix the mustard with 1 tablespoon cold water in a cup, add to the bowl, and mix to a firm dough with a blunt knife, adding a dash more water if the dough feels dry and crumbly. Wrap and chill for at least 30 minutes.

**Check** the fish for any stray bones, then cut into small chunks. Toss with the cornstarch in a small bowl and sprinkle into a shallow ovenproof dish or pie plate. Push the eggs down between the pieces of fish.

**Sprinkle** the scallions, peppercorns, parsley, and peas into the dish and spoon the sauce on top. Roll out the pastry dough on a lightly floured surface until slightly larger than the dish. Brush the rim of the dish with water and lay the pastry ove itr, trimming off the excess. Crimp the pastry edges and make a hole in the center. Brush with beaten egg and sprinkle with salt. Bake in a preheated oven, at 400°F, for 20 minutes. Reduce the temperature to 325°F and cook for 40 minutes, until the pastry is deep golden.

**For homemade Parmesan cheese sauce**, melt 3 tablespoons butter in a saucepan, add 1/3 cup all-purpose flour, and mix well over medium heat for 1 minute, making a paste. Remove from the heat and blend 1 1/2 cups milk into the paste. Return to the heat and cook, stirring, until the sauce is thick and bubbling. Beat in 3/4 cup shredded Parmesan cheese and season to taste. Transfer to a bowl and let cool.

# sea bass with sea asparagus

Serves **4**
Preparation time **20 minutes**
Cooking time **55 minutes**

6 **red-skinned** or **white round potatoes**, thinly sliced
⅓ cup **olive oil**
1 tablespoon chopped **thyme**
4 **sea bass** or **red snapper fillets**, about 5 oz each
3 oz **prosciutto**, chopped
2 **shallots**, finely chopped
finely grated rind of 1 **lemon**
8 oz **sea asparagus**
**salt** and **black pepper**

**Toss** the potato slices with ¼ cup of the oil, a little salt and black pepper, and the thyme in a bowl. Transfer to a roasting pan or ovenproof dish and spread out in an even layer. Cover with aluminum foil and bake in a preheated oven, at 375°F, for about 30 minutes, until the potatoes are tender.

**Score** the fish fillets with a sharp knife. Mix the prosciutto with the shallots, lemon rind, and a little black pepper and use to sandwich the fish fillets together. Tie at intervals with string. Cut each of the sandwiched fillets through the center to make 4 even portions.

**Lay** the fish over the potatoes and return to the oven, uncovered, for another 20 minutes or until the fish is cooked through.

**Sprinkle** the sea asparagus around the fish and drizzle with the remaining oil. Return to the oven for another 5 minutes before serving.

**For bacon-wrapped trout with potatoes**, bake the potatoes as above. Score 4 whole, descaled and gutted trout along each side and tuck several herb sprigs, such as parsley, tarragon, or dill, into the cavity of each fish. Wrap 2 smoked bacon slices around each fish and lay over the potato layer. Bake, uncovered, in the oven for another 25–30 minutes, until the bacon is crisp and the fish is cooked through.

# halibut with roasted vegetables

Serves **4**
Preparation time **25 minutes**
Cooking time **about 1 hour**

8 oz **shallots**
8 **small whole beets**, scrubbed and cut into wedges
1 1/4 lb **new potatoes**, scrubbed
1 small **fennel bulb**, trimmed and cut into wedges
1/2 cup **olive oil**
plenty of **rosemary sprigs**
8 **garlic cloves**, peeled
4 **halibut fillets**, about 5–6 oz each
6 **canned anchovy fillets**, drained
1 tablespoon **lemon juice**
2 tablespoons chopped **parsley**
**salt** and **black pepper**

**Put** the shallots into a heatproof bowl, cover with boiling water, and let stand for 2 minutes. Drain and rinse in cold water. Peel away the skins, leaving the shallots whole.

**Sprinkle** the shallots in a roasting pan with the beets, potatoes, and fennel. Drizzle with 3 tablespoons of the olive oil and roast in a preheated oven, at 425°F, for 45–50 minutes or until the vegetables are lightly roasted. Add the rosemary sprigs and garlic after half an hour of cooking.

**Season** the halibut on both sides and lay over the vegetables. Return the roasting pan to the oven for another 15 minutes or until the fish is cooked through.

**Chop** the anchovy fillets finely and whisk with the remaining olive oil, lemon juice, parsley, and a little salt and black pepper in a bowl to make a dressing.

**Pile** the halibut and vegetables onto warm serving plates and spoon the dressing over the fish to serve.

**For baked cod with anchovies & tomatoes**, heat 2 tablespoons olive oil in a roasting pan on the stove and sauté 1 small chopped red onion for 5 minutes, until softened. Add 2 teaspoons finely chopped rosemary, 6 drained and finely chopped canned anchovy fillets, 12 pitted ripe black olives, and 4 quartered tomatoes. Mix well. Season 4 chunky skinless cod fillets, about 6 oz each, and push down into the center of the pan. Drizzle with a little extra olive oil and bake in a preheated oven, at 375°F, for about 25 minutes, until the fish is cooked through.

# baked sardines with mozzarella

Serves **2**
Preparation time **10 minutes**
Cooking time **30 minutes**

1 **small onion**, finely chopped
2 **garlic cloves**, thinly sliced
1 **celery stick**, thinly sliced
3 tablespoons **extra virgin olive oil**
4 oz **piquillo peppers** from a jar or can, drained
1 tablespoon **capers**, rinsed and drained
4 **large filleted sardines**
4 oz **mozzarella cheese balls**
4 slices of **ciabatta**
**salt** and **black pepper**

**Place** the onion, garlic, and celery in a small roasting pan or ovenproof dish with 1 tablespoon of the oil. Mix well. Cook in a preheated oven, at 400°F, for 10 minutes, until softened.

**Slice** the piquillo peppers thinly and add to the roasting pan with the capers and season lightly with salt and black pepper. Lay the sardines on top and drizzle with another tablespoon of the oil. Return the roasting pan to the oven for another 15 minutes, until the sardines are cooked through.

**Add** the mozzarella to the roasting pan and return to the oven for a final 2 minutes.

**Toast** the ciabatta for 1–2 minutes on both sides.

**Arrange** the toasted ciabatta on warm serving plates and pile the sardines and vegetables on top. Serve drizzled with the pan juices and the remaining oil.

**For baked tuna with roasted vegetables**, cook the onion, garlic, and celery as above. Add 2 tuna steaks, about 4 oz each, and 1 cup sliced, drained roasted red peppers from a jar to the roasting pan and return to the oven for 10 minutes. Add 8 ripe black olives and a squeeze of lemon to the pan and return to the oven for another 2 minutes. Flake the tuna into pieces and pile onto toasted ciabatta with the vegetables as above, drizzling with another 1 tablespoon extra virgin olive oil.

# baked shrimp & fruit couscous

Serves **2**
Preparation time **20 minutes**
Cooking time **40 minutes**

8 oz **raw peeled shrimp**
1 large **onion**, chopped
1 **medium-strength green chile,** seeded and finely chopped
2 **garlic cloves**, thinly sliced
1 teaspoon **fennel seeds**
½ teaspoon **smoked paprika**
¼ cup **olive oil**
1 cup **couscous**
1 cup **hot fish** or **chicken stock** (see pages 178 and 36 for homemade)
⅓ cup **fresh cilantro**, chopped
1 cups sliced, drained **marinated artichokes**
2 **ripe peaches** or **nectarines**, pitted and sliced
**salt** and **black pepper**

**Pat** the shrimp dry between sheets of paper towels.

**Put** the onion, chile, garlic, fennel seeds, paprika, and oil into a shallow casserole and mix well. Cover and cook in a preheated oven, at 350°F, for 20 minutes, until the onions are soft.

**Add** the shrimp and return the casserole to the oven, uncovered, for another 15 minutes or until the shrimp have turned pink.

**Meanwhile,** put the couscous into a heatproof bowl and add the hot stock. Let stand for 5 minutes, until the stock has been absorbed.

**Fluff** the couscous up with a fork and add to the casserole with the cilantro, artichokes, and peaches or nectarines. Mix well and season to taste with salt and black pepper. Replace the lid and return to the oven for a final 5 minutes to heat through.

**For pesto shrimp with couscous**, put ⅓ cup pine nuts in a shallow casserole and toast in a preheated oven, at 350°F, for about 8–10 minutes. Transfer the pine nuts to a bowl. Cook the onion, garlic, and oil and then the shrimp in the casserole as above, omitting the chile, fennel seeds, and paprika. Prepare the couscous with the stock as above and add to the casserole with ⅓ cup store-bought green pesto, 2 pitted and sliced ripe peaches, ⅓ cup torn basil leaves, and the toasted pine nuts. Mix well and season to taste with salt and black pepper. Return to the oven for a final 5 minutes to heat through.

# smoked clam & bacon gratin

Serves **4**
Preparation time **25 minutes**
Cooking time about **1½ hours**

6 **red-skinned** or **white round potatoes**
1 (10 oz) **can smoked clams**, drained
3 oz **bacon slices**, finely diced
3 **shallots**, thinly sliced
1 cup **light cream**
1 cup **milk**
1 tablespoon chopped **thyme**
2 **garlic cloves**, crushed
½ cup shredded **Gruyère cheese**
1 cup **fresh white bread crumbs**
3 tablespoons **butter**, melted, plus extra for greasing
**black pepper**

**Grease** a 2½-quart shallow ovenproof dish. Scrub and thinly slice the potatoes, then layer half into the dish.

**Coarsely** chop the clams and sprinkle them over the potatoes with the bacon and shallots. Arrange the remaining potato slices on top.

**Beat** together the cream, milk, thyme, garlic, and half the Gruyère in a bowl. Season with plenty of black pepper and pour the sauce over the potatoes. Cover with aluminum foil and bake in a preheated oven, at 350°F, for 45 minutes.

**Stir** the bread crumbs into the melted butter until coated. Sprinkle them over the potatoes and sprinkle with the remaining Gruyère. Return to the oven, uncovered, for another 45–50 minutes, until the potatoes are tender and the topping is golden. Serve with a green or tomato salad, if liked.

**For roasted tomatoes with capers**, to serve as an accompaniment, halve 8 small ripe tomatoes and place, cut side up, in a roasting pan. Sprinkle with ½ teaspoon granulated sugar, a little salt and black pepper ,and 1 teaspoon dried oregano. Drizzle with 3 tablespoons olive oil and sprinkle with 2 tablespoons rinsed and drained capers. Bake in a preheated oven, at 350°F, for 50–60 minutes, until the tomatoes are tender and lightly browned.

# classic paella

Preparation time **40 minutes**
Cooking time about **1½ hours**
Serves **6**

2 lb **fresh mussels**
4 **garlic cloves**
1 small bunch of **mixed herbs**
⅔ cup **dry white wine**
8½ cups **hot chicken stock** (see page 36 for homemade) or **water**
¼ cup **olive oil**
4 **small cleaned squid**, cut into rings
1 large **onion**, finely chopped
1 **red bell pepper**, cored, seeded, and chopped
4 large **ripe tomatoes**, skinned (see page 11), seeded, and chopped
12 **skinless, boneless chicken thighs**, cut into bite-size pieces
2⅔ cups **paella rice**
large pinch of **saffron threads**, crumbled
1 cup **fresh** or **frozen peas**
12 large **peeled shrimp**
**salt** and **black pepper**

**Scrub** the mussels in cold water. Scrape off any barnacles and pull away the dark hairy beads. Discard any with damaged shells or open ones that do not close when tapped firmly with a knife. Set aside.

**Slice** 2 of the garlic cloves and crush the remainder. Place the sliced garlic in a large, heavy saucepan with the herbs, wine and ⅔ **cup** of the hot stock or water and season well with salt and black pepper. Add the mussels, cover, and cook, shaking the pan frequently, for 4–5 minutes, until all the shells have opened. Lift out with a slotted spoon into a bowl, discarding any that remain closed. Strain the cooking liquid and reserve.

**Heat** 2 tablespoons of the oil in the pan and sauté the squid, stirring frequently, for 5 minutes. Add the onion, red bell pepper, and crushed garlic and cook gently for 5 minutes, until softened. Add the mussel cooking liquid and tomatoes and season with salt and black pepper. Bring to a boil, then reduce the heat and cook gently, stirring, for 15–20 minutes, until thickened. Transfer to a bowl.

**Sauté** the chicken in the remaining oil in the pan for 5 minutes. Add the rice and cook, stirring, for 3 minutes. Return the squid mixture, add one-third of the remaining stock and the saffron, and bring to a boil, stirring. Cover and simmer, adding stock a little at a time, for 30 minutes or until the chicken is cooked, the rice is tender, and the liquid has been absorbed. Check the seasoning, add the peas and shrimp, and simmer, for 5 minutes, adding a little more stock, if required. Add the mussels, cover, and heat through for 5 minutes. Serve immediately.

# cod with oven fries & mint peas

Serves **4**
Preparation time **20 minutes**
Cooking time **1 hour 10 minutes**

4 **russet potatoes**
1/3 cup **vegetable oil**
good pinch each of **ground paprika, celery salt** and **ground cumin**
4 **chunky cod fillets**, about 5–6 oz each
1 1/2 tablespoons **butter**
2 2/3 cups **fresh** or **frozen peas**
1/2 cup **fish** or **chicken stock** (see pages 178 and 36 for homemade)
1 tablespoon chopped **mint**
2 tablespoons **crème fraîche** or **sour cream**
**salt** and **black pepper**

**Scrub** the potatoes and cut into 1/2 inch-thick slices. Cut across into chunky fries. Place in a bowl and drizzle with the oil, then turn in the oil until coated. Sprinkle with the paprika, celery salt, and cumin and mix.

**Heat** a large roasting pan in a preheated oven, at 400°F, for 3 minutes. Add the potatoes and spread out in an even layer. Bake in the oven for about 40 minutes, turning the potatoes a few times, until evenly pale golden.

**Season** the pieces of fish with salt and black pepper. Slide the potatoes to one side of the roasting pan and add the fish. Dot with the butter and return the roasting pan to the oven for another 20 minutes or until the fish is cooked through. Transfer the fish and oven fries to warm serving plates and return to the oven, with the door left open, to keep warm.

**Add** the peas and stock to the roasting pan and bring to a boil on the stove. Boil for 3 minutes or until the peas are tender. Transfer the contents of the roasting pan to a food processor, add the mint and crème fraîche or sour cream, and process to a puree. Serve with the fish and oven fries.

**For homemade ketchup**, to serve as an accompaniment, coarsely chop 5 ripe tomatoes and put in a saucepan with 1 coarsely chopped onion, 1/4 cup packed light brown sugar, 1/4 teaspoon cayenne pepper, 1/2 teaspoon salt, and 1/4 cup red wine vinegar. Bring to a boil, then reduce the heat and cook gently, stirring frequently, for about 30 minutes, until the sauce is thickened. Press through a strainer into a bowl. Let cool, then serve.

# squid with black rice

Serves **4**
Preparation time **20 minutes**
Cooking time **35 minutes**

1 lb **cleaned squid tubes**
¼ cup **olive oil**
1 **onion**, finely chopped
3 **garlic cloves**, crushed
1½ cups **paella rice**
½ oz **squid ink** (from your fish dealer or available online)
3¾ cups **fish** or **chicken stock** (see pages 178 and 36 for homemade)
2 teaspoons chopped **thyme**
⅔ cup **dry white wine**
¼ cup finely chopped **parsley**
**lime wedges**, for squeezing over, to serve
**salt** and **black pepper**

**Cut** the squid into ¼ inch-thick rings. Pat dry between several layers of paper towels. Heat the oil in a large saucepan and gently sauté the squid rings, half at a time, until they have turned opaque. Lift out onto a plate. Add the onion to the pan and sauté for 5 minutes, until softened, adding the garlic for the last couple of minutes. Stir in the rice and cook for 2 minutes, until coated in the oil and juices. Blend the squid ink with 2 tablespoons of the stock and set aside.

**Stir** the thyme and wine into the pan and cook quickly, stirring, until the wine has been absorbed. Pour in the remaining stock and bring to a boil. Reduce the heat to its lowest setting and cook, uncovered and stirring frequently, for about 20 minutes, until the rice is tender and the stock absorbed. Add more stock if too dry.

**Return** the squid to the pan and add the squid ink mixture and half the parsley. Stir well and season to taste with salt and black pepper. Ladle into bowls and sprinkle with remaining parsley. Serve with lime wedges.

**For red rice, saffron & seafood pilaf**, melt 3 tablespoons butter in a skillet and sauté 1 large finely chopped onion, 2 chopped celery sticks, and ½ cup toasted slivered almonds for 5 minutes. Rinse and drain 1¼ cups red rice and add to the pan with 2 cups stock, the grated rind of ½ orange, ½ teaspoon ground cumin, and ½ teaspoon crumbled saffron threads. Bring to a simmer and cook, stirring, for about 35–40 minutes, until tender, adding more stock if needed. Cut 12 oz monkfish or other firm-textured skinless white fish fillets into pieces and stir in the rice with some chopped cilantro. Cook through for a few minutes.

# lima bean & shrimp soup

Serves **4**
Preparation time **15 minutes,** plus overnight soaking
Cooking time **50 minutes**

1 ⅓ cups **dried lima beans**
1 lb **peeled shrimp**
½ teaspoon **hot chili powder**
2 tablespoons **olive oil**
¼ cup **tomato paste**
2 teaspoons **granulated sugar**
4 oz **bacon**, finely chopped
2 **onions**, coarsely chopped
3 **bay leaves**
**salt**
coarsely chopped **parsley**, to garnish

**Soak** the beans in a bowl of cold water overnight and then drain and rinse.

**Pat** the shrimp dry between several layers of paper towels. Dust lightly with the chili powder and a little salt.

**Heat** the oil in a large saucepan and sauté the shrimp briefly on both sides until they turn pink. Stir in the tomato paste, sugar, and 2 tablespoons water. Cook over gentle heat, stirring, for 1 minute, then scrape out onto a plate.

**Add** the bacon to the pan and cook until browned. Stir in the drained beans, onions, bay leaves, and 4 cups cold water and bring to a gentle simmer. Reduce the heat, cover, and cook gently for 40 minutes or until the beans are soft.

**Remove** the bay leaves. Blend the soup using an immersion blender or in a food processor. Return to the pan and reheat gently, stir in half the shrimp, and season to taste with salt and black pepper.

**Ladle** the soup into serving bowls and spoon the remaining shrimp and their cooking juices on top. Serve garnished with coarsely chopped parsley.

**For simple shrimp & pesto pasta**, bring a large saucepan of salted water to a boil. Add 12 oz dried tagliatelle and cook for 10 minutes, or according to the package directions, until the pasta is just tender. Drain lightly and return to the pan. Add 12 oz cooked, peeled shrimp, ¾ cup sun-dried tomato pesto, ¼ cup crème fraîche or Greek yogurt, and salt and black pepper to taste. Heat through gently for 2 minutes before serving.

# mussel & potato stew

Serves **2**
Preparation time **15 minutes**
Cooking time **30 minutes**

2 lb **fresh mussels**
2 tablespoons **butter**
1 **onion**, chopped
3 **garlic cloves**, crushed
⅔ cup **dry white wine**
1 lb **new potatoes**, scrubbed
1 cup coarsely chopped **curly parsley**
⅔ cup **light cream**
**salt** and **black pepper**

**Prepare** the mussels as described in the first step on page 142. Melt the butter in a large saucepan and gently sauté the onion for 5 minutes, until softened, adding the garlic for the last couple of minutes. Pour in the wine and bring to a boil. Add the mussels to the pan, cover, and cook, shaking the pan often, for 4–5 minutes, until all the shells are open. Lift out with a slotted spoon into a bowl.

**Add** the potatoes to the cooking juices in the pan, replace the lid, and cook gently for 15 minutes or until the potatoes are cooked through, adding a little water if the pan becomes dry. Meanwhile, remove two-thirds of the mussels from their shells, discarding any closed shells.

**Put** the parsley and cream into a food processor and process until the parsley is finely chopped. Pour into the pan. Bring to a boil and boil briefly until the juices have thickened slightly. Return all the mussels to the pan and heat through gently for a couple of minutes. Season with black pepper and a little salt and serve in bowls.

**For easy herb soda bread**, to serve alongside, mix 2 cups all-purpose flour, 2 cups whole-wheat flour, 1 teaspoon baking soda, and 1½ teaspoons salt in a bowl. Add 4 tablespoons butter, cubed, and rub in with fingertips until the mixture is like bread crumbs. Add 1 cup chopped herbs and 1 cup buttermilk and mix to a dough with a blunt knife. Transfer to a lightly floured surface, shape into a ball, and place on a greased baking sheet. Slash the top first in one direction and then the other. Bake in a preheated oven, at 425°F, for 30 minutes or until golden and the bottom sounds hollow when tapped.

# keralan seafood curry

Serves **4**
Preparation time **20 minutes**
Cooking time **35 minutes**

1½ lb **chunky skinless white fish fillets**, such as cod or pollock
3 tablespoons **vegetable oil**
1 tablespoon **yellow mustard seeds**
½ teaspoon **fenugreek seeds**
1 teaspoon **ground coriander**
1 **medium-strength green chile**, seeded and finely chopped
1 small **onion**, thinly sliced
3 **garlic cloves**, crushed
1½ inch piece of **fresh ginger root**, grated
½ teaspoon **ground turmeric**
1¾ cups **coconut milk**
¾ cup **canned diced tomatoes**
8 oz **cleaned squid tubes**, cut into thin rings
**salt**

**Check** the fish for any stray bones, then cut into chunky pieces.

**Heat** 2 tablespoons of the oil in a large, flameproof casserole or saucepan and gently cook the mustard and fenugreek seeds until they start to pop. Add the coriander, chile, and onion and cook gently, stirring, for 5 minutes.

**Stir** the garlic, ginger, and turmeric into the pan, then spoon the ingredients out onto a plate. Add the remaining oil to the pan and sauté the fish for 3–4 minutes, until browned on all sides, turning the pieces gently. Lift out with a slotted spoon onto a separate plate.

**Return** the spice mixture to the pan and add the coconut milk. Bring to a gentle simmer, cover, and cook for 10 minutes.

**Stir** in the tomatoes and return the fish to the pan with the squid. Cover and cook gently for another 10 minutes before serving in shallow bowls.

**For Keralan perfumed rice**, to serve alongside, rinse and drain 1½ cups basmati or other long-grain rice. Melt 2 tablespoons butter in a saucepan and gently cook 1 teaspoon cardamom pods, 1 halved cinnamon stick, several crumbled curry leaves, and 1 finely chopped shallot, stirring, for 3 minutes. Add the rice and cook, stirring, for 2 minutes. Pour in 2 cups water and bring to a boil. Reduce the heat to its lowest setting, cover, and cook for 12–15 minutes, or according to the package directions, until the rice is tender and the water has been absorbed. Fluff up the rice with a fork and season to taste with salt and black pepper to serve.

# salt cod minestrone

Serves **4**
Preparation time **20 minutes**, plus 1–2 days' soaking
Cooking time **50 minutes**

1 lb **salt cod**
¼ cup **olive oil**
2 **onions**, chopped
1 small **eggplant**, diced
3 **garlic cloves**, crushed
5 cups **fish stock** (see below for homemade)
2 tablespoons chopped **oregano**
2 tablespoons **tomato paste**
4 oz **dried spaghetti,** snapped into short lengths
2¾ cups quartered **cherry tomatoes**
6–8 large **green cabbage leaves** or **Tuscan kale,** finely shredded

**Soak** the salt cod in a bowl of cold water for 1–2 days, changing the water several times. Drain the cod and cut into small chunks, discarding any skin and bones.

**Heat** 2 tablespoons of the oil in a large saucepan and sauté the onions and eggplant gently, stirring frequently, for about 10 minutes, until lightly browned, adding the garlic for the last couple of minutes.

**Add** the stock to the pan and bring to a gentle simmer. Stir in the oregano, tomato paste, and salt cod, cover and cook gently for about 25 minutes, until the cod is tender.

**Stir** the spaghetti into the pan and cook for 5 minutes, until almost tender. Stir in the tomatoes and cabbage leaves and cook for another 5 minutes. Season to taste with salt and black pepper and serve in bowls.

**For homemade fish stock**, melt 1 tablespoon butter in a large saucepan and gently sauté 2 lb white fish bones and scraps until the scraps have turned opaque. Add a quartered onion, 2 coarsely chopped celery sticks, a handful of parsley, several lemon slices, and 1 teaspoon peppercorns. Cover with cold water and bring to a gentle simmer. Cook gently for 30–35 minutes. Strain through a strainer and let cool. Cover and chill for up to 2 days or freeze for up to 3 months.

# vegetarian

# masala dahl with sweet potato

Serves **4**
Preparation time **15 minutes**
Cooking time **50 minutes**

3 tablespoons **vegetable oil**
2 **onions**, chopped
2 **garlic cloves**, crushed
½ teaspoon **dried red pepper flakes**
¾ inch piece of **fresh ginger root**, grated
2 teaspoons **garam masala**
½ teaspoon **ground turmeric**
1 ¼ cups **dried split yellow peas**, rinsed and drained
¾ cup **canned diced tomatoes**
4 cups **vegetable stock** (see page 210 for homemade)
3 **sweet potatoes**, scrubbed and cut into small chunks
7 cups fresh **spinach**, washed and drained
**salt**
**naans**, to serve

**Heat** the oil in a saucepan and sauté the onions for 5 minutes. Add the garlic, red pepper flakes, ginger, garam masala, and turmeric and cook, stirring, for 2 minutes.

**Add** the split peas, tomatoes, and 3 cups of the stock and bring to a boil. Reduce the heat, cover, and cook gently for 20 minutes, until the peas have started to soften. Add more stock if the mixture becomes dry.

**Stir** in the sweet potatoes, replace the lid, and cook for another 20 minutes, until the potatoes and peas are tender, adding more stock if necessary to keep the dahl juicy. Add the spinach to the pan and stir until wilted. Add a little salt to taste. Serve with warmed naans (see below for homemade) and mango chutney.

**For homemade spiced naans**, to serve as an accompaniment, mix together 1¾ cups white bread flour, 1 teaspoon crushed coriander seeds, 1 teaspoon crushed cumin seeds,1 teaspoon salt, and 1 teaspoon active dry yeast in a bowl. Add 2 tablespoons plain yogurt and ½ cup warm milk and mix with a blunt knife to a soft dough, adding a dash more water if it feels dry. Knead on a lightly floured surface for 10 minutes (or use a freestanding mixer with dough hook attachment, kneading for 5 minutes). Turn into a bowl, cover with plastic wrap, and let rise for about 1 hour, until it has doubled in size. Turn out onto a floured surface and divide into 4 equal pieces. Roll out each into a tear shape about 8½ inches long. Heat a flat griddle pan or dry skillet until hot and cook the breads for 2–3 minutes on each side, until puffed and lightly browned.

# all-in-one vegetable breakfast

Serves **4**
Preparation time **10 minutes**
Cooking time **35 minutes**

2½ cups cubed **cooked potatoes**
¼ cup **olive oil**
few **thyme sprigs**
8 oz **button mushrooms**
12 **cherry tomatoes**
4 **eggs**
2 tablespoons chopped **parsley**, for sprinkling
**salt** and **black pepper**

**Spread** the potato cubes out in an even layer in a roasting pan. Drizzle with 2 tablespoons of the oil, sprinkle with the thyme sprigs, and season with salt and black pepper. Bake in a preheated oven, at 425°F, for 10 minutes.

**Stir** the potato cubes well, then add the mushrooms and return the roasting pan to the oven for another 10 minutes. Add the tomatoes and return the pan to the oven for another 10 minutes.

**Make** 4 hollows in between the vegetables and carefully break an egg into each hollow. Return the pan to the oven for a final 3–4 minutes, until the eggs are set.

**Sprinkle** the parsley over the top and serve straight from the pan.

**For all-in-one vegetable dinner**, without the eggs, cook the recipe above using 4 cups diced potatoes and 12 oz mushrooms. Then sprinkle 1 cup shredded cheddar cheese over the vegetables for the final 10 minutes of cooking.

# pappardelle with pea shoots & dill

Serves **2**
Preparation time **5 minutes**
Cooking time about
**12 minutes**

8 oz **dried papperdelle** or other ribbon pasta
4 tablespoons **butter**
1 **garlic clove**, crushed
2 tablespoons chopped **dill**
½ cup freshly grated **Parmesan cheese**
¾ cup **pea shoots**, thick stems discarded
**lemon wedges**, for squeezing over
**salt** and **black pepper**

**Bring** a large saucepan of salted water to a boil. Add the pasta and cook for 8–10 minutes, or according to the package directions, until just tender. Drain and return to the pan.

**Dot** the butter onto the hot pasta and add the garlic, dill, Parmesan, and a little salt and black pepper. Stir until well mixed, then add the pea shoots and stir until slightly wilted and distributed through the pasta.

**Serve** immediately with lemon wedges for squeezing over the pasta.

**For spaghetti carbonara with olives & basil**, beat together 1 whole egg, 2 egg yolks, ½ cup light cream, ½ cup freshly grated Parmesan cheese, 1 crushed garlic clove, and a little salt and black pepper in a bowl. Cook 8 oz dried spaghetti or linguini in a large saucepan of lightly salted boiling water for 8 minutes, or according to the package directions, until tender. Drain and return to the pan. Add the egg mixture and ½ cup chopped, pitted ripe black olives. Stir until the eggs are lightly cooked in the heat of the pasta, returning to the heat briefly, if necessary. Serve immediately, sprinkled with plenty of torn basil leaves.

# pesto & lemon soup

Serves **6**
Preparation time **10 minutes**
Cooking time **25 minutes**

1 tablespoon **olive oil**
1 **onion**, finely chopped
2 **garlic cloves**, finely chopped
2 **tomatoes**, skinned (see page 11) and chopped
5 cups **vegetable stock** (see page 210 for homemade)
1 tablespoons **store-bought pesto**, plus extra to serve
grated rind and juice of 1 **lemon**
1½ cups small **broccoli** florets and sliced stems
1 **zucchini**, diced
⅔ cup **frozen shelled edamame** (soybeans)
3 oz **small dried pasta shapes**
1 cup washed, drained, and shredded **spinach**
**salt** and **black pepper**
**basil leaves**, to garnish (optional)
**sun-dried tomato focaccia** or **ciabatta**, to serve

**Heat** the oil in a saucepan and gently sauté the onion for 5 minutes, until softened. Add the garlic, tomatoes, stock, pesto, lemon rind, and a little salt and black pepper and simmer gently for 10 minutes.

**Add** the broccoli, zucchini, edamame, and pasta shapes and simmer for 6 minutes.

**Stir** the spinach and lemon juice into the pan and cook for 2 minutes, until the spinach has just wilted and the pasta is just tender.

**Ladle** the soup into bowls, top with extra spoonfuls of pesto, and garnish with a few basil leaves, if desired. Serve with warmed olive or sun-dried tomato focaccia or ciabatta bread.

**For homemade Parmesan thins**, to serve as an alternative accompaniment to the bread, line a baking sheet with nonstick parchment paper and sprinkle 1¼ cups freshly grated Parmesan cheese into 18 well-spaced mounds onto the lined baking sheet. Bake in a preheated oven, at 375°F, for 5 minutes or until the cheese has melted and is just beginning to brown. Let cool and harden, then peel off the lining paper and serve the thins on the side with the soup.

# bell pepper stew & cheese toasts

Serves **4**
Preparation time **25 minutes**
Cooking time **50 minutes**

1/3 cup **olive oil**
6 **mixed red**, **green**, and **orange bell peppers**, cored, seeded, and cubed
1 **onion**, thinly sliced
1 large **fennel bulb**, trimmed and thinly sliced
3 **garlic cloves**, crushed
2 (14½ oz) **cans diced tomatoes**
1¼ cups **vegetable stock** (see page 210)
1 tablespoon packed **light brown sugar**
¼ cup **tomato paste**
2 teaspoons **ground paprika**
2 teaspoons **fennel seeds**, lightly crushed
**salt**

**Toasts**
2 **panini breads**
2 tablespoons **olive oil**
2 teaspoons **capers**
4 oz **goat cheese**
2 tablespoons chopped **lovage** or **basil**

**Heat** the oil in a large, heavy skillet and gently sauté the bell peppers, onion, and fennel slices, stirring frequently, for 20–25 minutes, until the vegetables are soft and lightly browned.

**Stir** in the garlic, tomatoes, stock, sugar, tomato paste, paprika, and fennel seeds and bring to a boil. Reduce the heat, cover with a lid or aluminum foil, and simmer gently for another 20 minutes, until the stew is thick and pulpy. Season to taste with a little salt.

**Slice** the panini breads in half and drizzle the cut sides with the oil. Rinse and drain the capers. Slice the goat cheese and use with the capers and lovage or basil to sandwich the breads together. Heat a large, dry skillet or ridged grill pan until hot and cook for 2–3 minutes on each side until browned, pressing the breads down with a spatula to flatten. Cut into chunky pieces and serve with the pepper stew.

**For cheese & lovage dumplings**, to serve as an alternative accompaniment to the toasts, mix together 1⅔ cups all-purpose flour, 1½ teaspons baking powder, ½ cup vegetable shortening, ¾ cup shredded sharp cheddar cheese, and 2 tablespoons chopped lovage in a bowl. Add a little salt and black pepper and ⅔ cup cold water and mix with a blunt knife to a soft dough. Divide the dough into 8 pieces and shape each into a ball. Add to the cooked stew and cover with a lid or tented aluminum foil to trap the steam. Cook for 20 minutes, until the dumplings are light and fluffy.

# warm greek salad

Serves **4**
Preparation time **10 minutes**
Cooking time **25 minutes**

8 **ripe tomatoes**, coarsely chopped
2 **green bell peppers**, cored, seeded, and coarsely chopped
1 small **red onion**, thinly sliced
2 **garlic cloves**, crushed
2 tablespoons chopped **oregano**
⅓ cup **extra virgin olive oil**
8 oz **feta cheese**
12 **pitted ripe black olives**
**salt** and **black pepper**
**pita breads**, to serve

**Sprinkle** the tomatoes, green bell peppers, and onion in a shallow ovenproof dish.

**Mix** the garlic with the oregano, oil, plenty of black pepper, and a little salt. Drizzle the mixture over the vegetables. Bake in a preheated oven, at 400°F, for 10 minutes.

**Crumble** the feta into small pieces and sprinkle it over the vegetables along with the olives. Return the dish to the oven for another 15 minutes. Serve warm with toasted pita breads.

**For garlic bread sauce**, to serve alongside, tear a small pita bread into pieces and place in a bowl with ⅓ cup milk. Let stand for 5 minutes, until the bread has softened. Lift the bread out of the bowl and squeeze out the excess milk. Place the bread in a food processor and add 2 crushed garlic cloves and ¼ cup olive oil. Process to a smooth paste. Add another ¼ cup oil and 2 tablespoons white wine vinegar and process again to a paste. Season to taste with salt and black pepper and transfer to a serving bowl. Cover and chill until ready to serve.

# green bean & potato stew

Serves **4**
Preparation time **25 minutes**
Cooking time **50 minutes**

2 cups halved, trimmed **green beans**
3½ cups thinly sliced, trimmed **string beans** (or extra green beans)
1 cup **shelled baby fava beans**, thawed if frozen
2 tablespoons **olive oil**
1 large **onion**, finely chopped
6 **red-skinned** or **white round potatoes**, cut into small chunks
4 **garlic cloves**, crushed
2 tablespoons **sherry vinegar**
2 tablespoons **whole-grain mustard**
2 tablespoons packed **light brown sugar**
2 **bay leaves**
1 (14½ oz) **can diced tomatoes**
3 tablespoons **sun-dried tomato paste**
**salt** and **black pepper**

**Bring** a large saucepan of water to a boil. Add the green and string beans and cook for 5 minutes. Add the fava beans and cook for another 1 minute. Drain and set aside. Wipe out the pan.

**Heat** the oil in the pan and gently sauté the onion and potatoes, turning frequently, for 5 minutes. Cover and cook gently for another 10 minutes or until the potatoes are softened and beginning to brown.

**Stir** in the garlic, vinegar, mustard, sugar, bay leaves, tomatoes, and tomato paste. Bring to a boil, then reduce and gently simmer, uncovered and stirring frequently, for 15 minutes, until the sauce is thick.

**Add** all the beans to the pan and stir well. Heat through gently for 10 minutes, adding a dash of water to the pan if the mixture becomes dry. Season to taste with salt and black pepper before serving.

**For Catalonian ratatouille**, to serve with the green bean and potato stew, heat 2 tablespoons olive oil in a large saucepan or skillet and gently sauté 1 large diced eggplant for 5 minutes. Add 3 cored, seeded, and diced red bell peppers, 1 chopped onion, and another 2 tablespoons oil. Cook gently, stirring, for 5 minutes. Add 2 crushed garlic cloves, 5 skinned and chopped tomatoes, and a little salt and black pepper. Cover and cook gently for 10 minutes. Stir well and cook, uncovered, for another few minutes, if necessary, until the stew is thick and pulpy. Serve with warmed bread.

# fig, goat cheese & tapenade tart

Serves **4**
Preparation time **10 minutes**
Cooking time **20–25 minutes**

1 sheet **ready-to-bake puff pastry**, defrosted if frozen
**all-purpose flour**, for dusting
**beaten egg**, to glaze
3 tablespoons store-bought or homeade **olive tapenade** (see page 122)
3 **ripe figs**, quartered
6 **cherry tomatoes**, halved
4 oz **soft goat cheese**, crumbled
2 teaspoons chopped **thyme**
2 tablespoons freshly grated **Parmesan cheese**

**Roll** out the pastry on a lightly floured surface until ⅛ inch thick into a rectangle 8 x 12 inches, trimming the edges.

**Prick** the pastry with a fork and score a border 1 inch in from the edges. Transfer to a baking sheet. Brush the pastry with beaten egg to glaze and bake in a preheated oven, at 400°F, for 12–15 minutes.

**Remove** the pastry from the oven and carefully press down the center to flatten slightly. Spread the center with the tapenade and then arrange the figs, tomatoes, goat cheese, thyme, and Parmesan over the top.

**Return** the tart to the oven for another 5–10 minutes, until the pastry is lightly browned, the cheese has melted, and the figs are cooked. Brown the top under a preheated hot broiler, if desired, making sure that the pastry edges don't burn (you can cover them with aluminum foil). Serve warm with a leafy green salad, if desired.

**For roasted vegetable & goat cheese tart**, thinly slice 1 zucchini and 1 eggplant, core, seed, and quarter 1 red bell pepper, and cut 1 red onion into thin wedges. Brush the vegetables with olive oil and cook under a preheated hot broiler for 3–4 minutes on each side until tender. Cook the recipe above using the roasted vegetables instead of the figs and tomatoes.

# blackened tofu with fried rice

Serves **2**
Preparation time **25 minutes**, plus marinating
Cooking time **20 minutes**

1 **hot green chile,** seeded and coarsely chopped
1½ inch **fresh ginger root**, peeled and coarsely chopped
2 **garlic cloves**, coarsely chopped
2 tablespoons packed **dark brown sugar**
3 tablespoons **soy sauce**
7 oz **firm tofu**
3 tablespoons **vegetable oil** or **wok** or **stir-fry oil**
1 bunch of **scallions**, chopped
12 **baby corn**, cut diagonally into ½ inch slices
1½ cups shredded **napa cabbage**
1 (9 oz) **package precooked white long-grain rice** or 1¾ cups **cold cooked rice**
⅓ cup chopped **fresh cilantro**

**Blend** the chile, ginger, garlic, sugar, and 2 tablespoons soy sauce in a small food processor to a loose paste. Drain the tofu and pat dry on paper towels. Cut into chunks. Mix with the chile paste in a nonmetallic bowl, then cover and let marinate for 1–2 hours.

**Heat** 1 tablespoon of the oil in a skillet or shallow flameproof casserole over high heat. When hot, tip in the tofu mixture and sauté quickly, turning occasionally, for 5 minutes, until browned on all sides. Lift out with a slotted spoon onto a plate.

**Add** the remaining oil to the pan, stir in the scallions and corn, and stir-fry for 3–4 minutes, until beginning to brown. Add the cabbage and stir-fry for 2 minutes. Add the rice and cilantro and stir-fry for another 5 minutes, until the rice is thoroughly hot. Drizzle with the remaining soy sauce, stir in the cilantro, and sprinkle with the tofu. Cook for another 1 minute.

**For herb & lentil pilaf**, heat 3 tablespoons vegetable oil in a skillet or shallow flameproof casserole and gently sauté 1 chopped onion and 2 chopped celery sticks until softened. Add 1 teaspoon crushed cumin seeds, 1 halved cinnamon stick, and 1 teaspoon mild chili powder. Cook, stirring, for 2 minutes. Stir in 3 cups vegetable stock and bring to a boil. Add 1 cup rinsed and drained dried green lentils and cook gently for 5 minutes. Add 1 cup uncooked white long-grain rice and cook for 12–15 minutes, or according to the package directions until both rice and lentils are tender, adding a little more stock if the mixture becomes dry. Drizzle with the juice of 1 lime and stir in ⅓ cup chopped parsley and ¼ cup chopped cilantro before serving.

# okra & coconut stew

Serves **3–4**
Preparation time **15 minutes**
Cooking time **40 minutes**

12 oz **okra**
¼ cup **vegetable oil**
2 **onions**, chopped
2 **green bell peppers**, cored, seeded and cut into chunks
3 **celery sticks**, thinly sliced
3 **garlic cloves**, crushed
4 teaspoons **Cajun spice blend**
½ teaspoon **ground turmeric**
1¼ cups **vegetable stock** (see page 210 for homemade)
1¾ cups **coconut milk**
1⅓ cups **frozen corn kernels**
juice of 1 **lime**
¼ cup chopped **fresh cilantro**
**salt** and **black pepper**

**Trim** the stem ends from the okra and cut the pods into ¾ inch lengths.

**Heat** 2 tablespoons of the oil in a large, deep skillet or shallow, flameproof casserole and sauté the okra for 5 minutes. Lift out with a slotted spoon onto a plate.

**Add** the remaining oil to the skillet and gently sauté the onions, bell peppers, and celery, stirring frequently, for 10 minutes, until softened but not browned. Add the garlic, spice blend, and turmeric and cook for 1 minute.

**Pour** in the stock and coconut milk and bring to a boil. Reduce the heat, cover, and cook gently for 10 minutes. Return the okra to the pan with the corn kernels, lime juice, and cilantro and cook for another 10 minutes. Season to taste with salt and black pepper and serve.

**For easy corn bread**, to serve as an accompaniment, mix together 1 cup cornmeal, ¾ cup all-purpose flour, 1 teaspoon salt, 2 teaspoons baking powder, ½ teaspoon ground cumin, and ½ teaspoon dried red pepper flakes in a bowl. Beat 1 egg with 1 cup milk and add to the bowl. Mix gently until just combined (do not overmix). Turn into a greased 8½ x 4½ x 2½ inch loaf pan. Bake in a preheated oven, at 375°F, for 30 minutes, until firm to the touch. Serve warm or transfer to a wire rack to cool.

# sicilian caponata

Serves **4**
Preparation time **15 minutes**, plus standing
Cooking time **30 minutes**

½ cup **olive oil**
2 **eggplants**, cut into 1½ inch cubes
1 large **onion**, coarsely chopped
3 **celery sticks**, sliced
⅓ cup **pine nuts**
2 **garlic cloves**, chopped
1 (14½ oz) **can plum tomatoes**, drained and coarsely chopped
2 tablespoons **capers**, rinsed and drained
½ cup **pitted green olives**
3 tablespoons **red wine vinegar**
1 tablespoon **granulated sugar**
6 **basil leaves**
**salt** and **black pepper**
**crusty bread**, to serve

**Heat** the oil in a large skillet over high heat until the oil begins to shimmer and sauté the eggplants, in two batches, stirring frequently, for 5–6 minutes, until golden and tender, lifting out with a slotted spoon into a bowl.

**Pour** off all but 2 tablespoons of the oil from the skillet. Add the onion, celery, and pine nuts and gently sauté for 10 minutes, until the vegetables are softened and lightly golden. Return the eggplants to the skillet and stir in all the remaining ingredients except the basil. Season to taste with salt and black pepper.

**Bring** to a boil, then reduce the heat and simmer for 5 minutes. Stir in the basil. Remove from the heat and let stand for at least 15 minutes to let the flavors develop.

**Serve** warm or cold, as an antipasto, side dish, or a vegetarian main dish, with some crusty bread on the side.

**For potato & red pepper caponata**, peel and cut 4 red-skinned or white round potatoes into 1½ inch cubes. Cook in a saucepan of salted boiling water until tender, then drain. Heat ¼ cup olive oil in a skillet and gently sauté the onion, celery, and pine nuts as above, along with 2 red bell peppers, cored, seeded, and cut into large chunks. Toss in the potatoes and the remaining ingredients as above, using ½ cup ripe black olives instead of the green olives. Season to taste with salt and black pepper and finish cooking as above.

# asparagus & new potato tortilla

Serves **4**
Preparation time **15 minutes**
Cooking time **40 minutes**

12 oz **asparagus spears**
12 oz **new potatoes**
½ cup **olive oil**
1 **onion**, chopped
6 **eggs**
2 tablespoons torn **basil leaves**
**salt** and **black pepper**

**Snap** off the woody ends of the asparagus and cut the spears into 2 inch lengths. Slice the potatoes thinly.

**Heat** ¼ cup of the oil in a sturdy 10 inch-diameter skillet. Add the asparagus and sauté gently for 5 minutes, until slightly softened. Lift out with a slotted spoon onto a plate. Add the remaining oil to the skillet and add the potatoes and onion. Cook gently, turning frequently in the oil, for about 15 minutes, until the potatoes are tender.

**Beat** the eggs with a little salt and black pepper in a bowl and stir in the basil leaves. Add the asparagus to the skillet and combine the vegetables so that they are fairly evenly distributed. Pour the egg mixture over the vegetables and reduce the heat to its lowest setting. Cover with a lid or aluminum foil and cook for about 10 minutes, until almost set but still a little wobbly in the center.

**Loosen** the edge of the tortilla, cover the skillet with a plate, and invert the tortilla onto it. Slide back into the skillet and return to the heat for 2–3 minutes, until the bottom is firm. Slide onto a clean plate and serve warm or cold, cut into wedges.

**For hollandaise sauce**, to spoon over the tortilla, put 1 tablespoon white wine vinegar in a food processor with 2 egg yolks. Blend lightly to combine. Cut 1¼ sticks butter into pieces and melt gently in a small saucepan. With the machine running, slowly pour in the melted butter until thick and smooth. Season to taste with salt and black pepper and add a dash of hot water if the sauce is too thick.

# spiced chickpeas with kale

Serves **4**
Preparation time **10 minutes**
Cooking time **35 minutes**

3 tablespoons **vegetable oil**
3 **red onions**, cut into wedges
2 tablespoons **mild curry paste**
1 (14½ oz) **can diced tomatoes**
1 (15 oz) **can chickpeas**, drained and rinsed
1¼ cups **vegetable stock** (see page 210 for homemade)
2 teaspoons backed **light brown sugar**
1½ cups chopped **curly kale**
**salt** and **black pepper**

**Heat** the oil in a large saucepan and sauté the onions for 5 minutes, until they are beginning to brown. Stir in the curry paste and then the tomatoes, chickpeas, stock, and sugar.

**Bring** to a boil, then reduce the heat, cover, and simmer gently for 20 minutes.

**Stir** in the kale and cook gently for another 10 minutes. Season to taste with salt and black pepper and serve.

**For sesame flatbreads**, to serve as an accompaniment, put 2 cups all-purpose flour, 1 teaspoon salt, and 3 tablespoons sesame seeds in a bowl. Add 3 tablespoons vegetable oil and ½ cup cold water and mix with a blunt knife to form a dough, adding a dash more water if the dough feels dry. Divide into 8 pieces and thinly roll out each piece on a lightly floured surface until about ⅛ inch thick. Heat a flat griddle or large dry skillet until hot and cook the flatbreads for about 2 minutes on each side, until pale golden. Serve warm.

# squash, kale & mixed bean soup

Serves **6**
Preparation time **15 minutes**
Cooking time **45 minutes**

1 tablespoon **olive oil**
1 **onion**, finely chopped
2 **garlic cloves**, finely chopped
1 teaspoon **smoked paprika**
½ **butternut squash**, peeled, seeded, and diced
2 small **carrots**, diced
4 **tomatoes**, skinned (optional, see page 11) and coarsely chopped
2 cups drained, **canned mixed beans**, such as kidney beans, pinto beans, and chickpeas
3¾ cups **vegetable stock** (see page 210 for homemade)
⅔ cup **crème fraîche** or **heavy cream**
1½ cups chopped **kale**
**salt** and **black pepper**
**focaccia,** to serve

**Heat** the oil in a saucepan and gently sauté the onion for 5 minutes, until it is softened. Stir in the garlic and smoked paprika and cook briefly, stirring, then add the squash, carrots, tomatoes, and beans.

**Pour** the stock into the pan, season to taste with salt and black pepper, and bring to a boil, stirring. Cover and simmer for 25 minutes or until the vegetables are tender.

**Stir** the crème fraîche or heavy cream into the soup, then add the kale, pressing it just beneath the surface of the stock. Replace the lid and cook for 5 minutes, until the kale has just wilted.

**Ladle** into bowls and serve with warm focaccia.

**For cheesy squash, red pepper & mixed bean soup**, sauté the onion in the oil, then add the garlic, smoked paprika, squash, tomatoes, and beans as above, adding a cored, seeded, and diced red bell pepper instead of the carrots. Pour in the stock, then add a 2½ inch piece of Parmesan rind and season to taste with salt and black pepper. Cover and simmer for 25 minutes. Stir in the crème fraîche or heavy cream as above but omit the kale. Discard the Parmesan rind, ladle the soup into bowls, and top with freshly grated Parmesan to serve.

# artichoke & barley risotto

Serves **4**
Preparation time **25 minutes**
Cooking time **45 minutes**

13 oz **Jerusalem artichokes**
4 tablespoons **butter**
1½ cups **pearl barley**
⅔ cup **dry white wine**
2 cups **hot vegetable stock** (see below for homemade)
4 oz **mascarpone cheese**
1 cup chopped **mixed herbs**, such as chives, parsley, tarragon, and dill
finely grated rind of 2 **lemons**
freshly grated **Parmesan cheese**, for sprinkling
**salt** and **black pepper**

**Scrub** and thinly slice the artichokes. Melt the butter in a large saucepan and gently sauté the artichokes, stirring, for 10 minutes, until beginning to soften.

**Add** the pearl barley and cook, stirring, for 2 minutes. Stir in the wine and cook quickly for 2–3 minutes, until the wine has been absorbed. Gradually add the hot stock to the pan, a ladleful at a time, and cook, stirring frequently, until each ladleful has been absorbed. Continue to cook, adding a ladleful of stock at a time and stirring frequently until each ladleful has mostly been absorbed before adding the next. This should take about 20–25 minutes, by which time the barley should be tender but retaining a little bite. Add a little more stock, if needed.

**Stir** the mascarpone, herbs, and lemon rind into the risotto and cook for another 2 minutes. Season to taste with salt and black pepper and serve sprinkled with grated Parmesan.

**For homemade vegetable stock**, heat 1 tablespoon vegetable oil in a large saucepan and gently sauté 2 washed, unpeeled, and coarsely chopped onions, 2 coarsely chopped carrots, 2 each coarsely chopped celery sticks, parsnips, and zucchini, and 3 cups sliced mushrooms, stirring frequently, for 10 minutes, until softened. Add 3 bay leaves and a handful of parsley and thyme sprigs. Cover with 6 cups cold water and bring to a boil. Reduce the heat and simmer gently, uncovered, for 40 minutes. Strain through a strainer and let cool. Cover and store in the refrigerator for up to several days or freeze for up to 6 months.

# carrot, lentil & tahini soup

Serves **4**
Preparation time **10 minutes**
Cooking time **45 minutes**

2 tablespoons **sesame seeds**, plus extra for sprinkling
2 tablespoons **olive oil**
1 **onion**, chopped
8 **carrots**, chopped
4 cups **vegetable stock** (see page 210 for homemade)
2 teaspoons chopped **lemon thyme leaves**, plus extra for sprinkling
¾ cup **dried green lentils**, rinsed and drained
⅓ cup **tahini paste**
**crème fraîche** or **Greek yogurt**, for topping
**salt** and **black pepper**

**Heat** the sesame seeds in a large, dry saucepan until lightly toasted. Transfer to a small bowl.

**Add** the oil to the pan and gently sauté the onion and carrots for 10 minutes, until softened. Add the stock and thyme and bring to a boil. Reduce the heat, cover, and cook gently for 10 minutes.

**Add** the lentils, cover, and cook gently for another 20 minutes or until the lentils are soft. Remove from the heat, let stand for 5 minutes, and then and stir in the tahini paste. Season to taste with salt and black pepper.

**Ladle** into bowls and top with spoonfuls of crème fraîche or Greek yogurt. Serve sprinkled with extra sesame seeds and thyme.

**For garlic-fried pita breads**, to serve as an accompaniment, slice 4 regular pita breads horizontally through the centers to make 8 thin slices. Whisk together ¼ cup olive oil, 1 crushed garlic clove, ½ teaspoon crushed fennel seeds, and a little salt and black pepper in a small bowl. Brush over both sides of the pita breads. Heat a flat griddle pan or large, dry skillet until hot and cook the breads for a couple of minutes on each side until pale golden and crisp. Serve warm with the soup.

# provençal vegetable stew

Serves **4**
Preparation time **15 minutes**
Cooking time **55 minutes**

¼ cup **olive oil**, plus extra for drizzling
1 large **red onion**, sliced
4 **garlic cloves**, chopped
2 teaspoons **ground coriander**
1 tablespoon chopped **thyme**
1 **fennel bulb**, trimmed and sliced
1 **red bell pepper**, cored, seeded, and sliced
4 **vine-ripened tomatoes**, diced
1¼ cups **vegetable stock** (see page 210 for homemade)
12 cup **Niçoise olives**
2 tablespoons chopped **parsley**
slices of **crusty bread**, to serve
**salt** and **black pepper**

**Heat** the oil in a large saucepan and gently sauté the onion, garlic, coriander, and thyme, stirring frequently, for 5 minutes, until the onion is softened. Add the fennel and red bell pepper and cook, stirring frequently, for 10 minutes, until softened.

**Stir** in the tomatoes and stock and season to taste with salt and black pepper. Bring to a boil, then reduce the heat, cover, and simmer gently for 30 minutes.

**Add** the olives and parsley to the pan and simmer, uncovered, for another 10 minutes.

**Meanwhile,** heat a ridged grill pan until hot and cook the bread slices until toasted and lightly charred on both sides. Drizzle liberally with oil.

**Serve** the stew hot with the toasted bread slices.

**For pasta with Provençal sauce**, cook the stew as above. Toward the end of the cooking time, cook 1 lb dried penne in a large saucepan of lightly salted boiling water for 10–12 minutes, or according to the package directions, until just tender. Drain well and serve the pasta topped with the vegetable stew as a pasta sauce, sprinkled with freshly grated Parmesan cheese and basil leaves.

# parsnip, sage & chestnut soup

Serves **4**
Preparation time **15 minutes**
Cooking time **50 minutes**

3 tablespoons store-bought or homemade **chili oil** (see below for homemade), plus extra for drizzling
40 **sage leaves**
1 **leek**, trimmed, cleaned and chopped
4 **parsnips**, coarsely chopped
5 cups **vegetable stock** (see page 210 for homemade)
pinch of **ground cloves**
1 (7 oz) **package cooked peeled chestnuts**
2 tablespoons **lemon juice**
**crème fraîche** or **Greek yogurt**, for topping
**salt** and **black pepper**

**Heat** the chili oil in a large saucepan until a sage leaf sizzles and crisps in 15–20 seconds, then sauté the remaining leaves, in batches, until crisp, lifting out with a slotted spoon onto a plate lined with paper towels. Set aside.

**Add** the leek and parsnips to the pan and sauté gently for 10 minutes, until softened. Add the stock and cloves and bring to a boil. Reduce the heat, cover, and cook gently for 30 minutes, until the vegetables are soft. Stir in the chestnuts and cook for another 5 minutes.

**Blend** the soup using an immersion blender or in a food processor. Add the lemon juice and reheat gently, seasoning to taste with salt and black pepper.

**Ladle** into bowls, top with a little crème fraîche or Greek yogurt, and drizzle sparingly with extra chili oil. Serve sprinkled with the sage leaves.

**For homemade chili oil**, pour 1¼ cups olive oil into a saucepan. Add 6 whole dried chiles, 2 bay leaves, and 1 rosemary sprig and heat through gently for 3 minutes. Remove from the heat and let cool completely. Using a pitcher or funnel, pour into a thoroughly clean glass canning jar or bottle, adding the chiles and herbs. Cover and store in a cool place for a week before using. The oil will become hotter during storage. Use as above, or in pasta and pizza recipes or any dishes where you want to add a little heat.

# barley, beer & mushroom cobbler

Serves **4**
Preparation time **30 minutes**
Cooking time about **1¾ hours**

4 tablespoons **butter**
1 lb **button mushrooms**, thickly sliced
1 large **onion**, sliced
1 small **rutabaga** or **sweet potato**, peeled and diced
1 tablespoon **all-purpose flour**
1¾ cups **strong ale**
1¼ cups **vegetable stock** (see page 210 for homemade)
⅓ cup **pearl barley**
2 tablespoons **whole-grain mustard**
1 tablespoon chopped **rosemary**
¼ cup **light cream**

**Cobbler**
1⅓ cups **all-purpose flour**, plus extra for dusting
1 teaspoon **baking powder**
1 stick **slightly salted butter**, cut into small pieces
¾ cup shredded **Gruyère cheese**
¼ cup **milk**, plus extra to glaze

**Melt** half the butter in a flameproof casserole and sauté the mushrooms for 10 minutes. Lift out and set aside. Melt the remaining butter in the casserole and sauté the onion and rutabaga or sweet potato for 8–10 minutes, until beginning to brown. Add the flour and cook, stirring, for 1 minute. Blend in the ale, then the stock. Bring to a boil and add the pearl barley, mustard, and rosemary. Cover and cook in a preheated oven, at 350°F, for 50 minutes–1 hour, until the barley is tender.

**Make** the cobbler. Put the flour and baking powder into a food processor, add the butter, and process until the mixture resembles bread crumbs. Add the Gruyère and milk and process to a thick dough, adding a dash more milk if dry. Transfer to a floured surface and roll out to ¾ inch thick. Cut out circles, using a 1¾ inch cutter, rerolling the scraps. Increase the oven temperature to 425°F. Stir the mushrooms and cream into the casserole and check the seasoning. Arrange the biscuits around the edge and brush with milk. Return to the oven, uncovered, for 20–25 minutes, until golden.

**For cauliflower & celeriac cobbler,** melt 2 tablespoons butter in a flameproof casserole and sauté 1 large sliced onion until softened. Add 1 large cauliflower, cut into florets, 1 peeled and diced celeriac, 2 teaspoons crushed cumin seeds, ½ teaspoon celery salt, and ¼ teaspoon cayenne pepper. Sauté gently for 5 minutes. Add 2 tablespoons flour and cook, stirring, for 1 minute. Remove from the heat and blend in 3 cups vegetable stock. Bring to a boil, cover, and cook as above, adding the cream and finishing with the biscuit topping. Sprinkle with chopped parsley and serve.

# spiced black beans & cabbage

Serves **2**
Preparation time **15 minutes**
Cooking time **30 minutes**

3 tablespoons **butter**
1 large **onion**, chopped
10 **baby carrots**, scrubbed
1 tablespoon store-bought or homemade **ras el hanout** spice blend (see below for homemade)
2 cups **vegetable stock** (see page 210 for homemade)
8 oz **new potatoes**, scrubbed and diced
1 (15 oz) **can black beans**, rinsed and drained
2 cups shredded **cabbage** or **collard greens**
**salt** (optional)

**Melt** the butter in a saucepan and gently sauté the onion and carrots for 5 minutes, until the onion is softened. Add the spice blend and sauté for 1 minute.

**Pour** in the stock and bring to a boil. Reduce the heat to its lowest setting and stir in the potatoes and beans. Cover and cook gently for 15 minutes, until the vegetables are tender and the juices slightly thickened.

**Add** the shredded cabbage or collard greens to the pan and cook for another 5 minutes. Season with salt, if necessary, and serve.

**For homemade ras el hanout spice blend**, put ½ teaspoon each cumin, coriander, and fennel seeds in a mortar and crush with a pestle. Add 1 teaspoon yellow mustard seeds and ¼ teaspoon each ground cinnamon and cloves and grind the spices together. Alternatively, use a small coffee or spice grinder to grind the spices.

# baked vegetables & mascarpone

Serve **4**
Preparation time **15 minutes**
Cooking time **1¾ hours**

6 tablespoons **butter**
2 **fennel bulbs**
1 tablespoon **lemon juice**
2 **zucchini**, sliced
8 oz **mascarpone cheese**
4 **eggs**
**2 garlic cloves**, crushed
1 cup shredded **Emmental cheese** or **Swiss cheese**
150 ml (¼ pint) **milk**
2 tablespoons chopped **parsley**
**salt** and **black pepper**

**Sprinkle** the butter in a shallow 2 quart ovenproof dish and put into a preheated oven, at 350°F, for 5 minutes, until melted. Meanwhile, chop the fennel, reserving the leafy tops. Toss the fennel in the melted butter, drizzle with the lemon juice, and season with salt and black pepper. Mix well. Cover and bake for 40 minutes.

**Add** the zucchini and stir the ingredients together. Return to the oven, uncovered, for another 30 minutes. Beat the mascarpone with the eggs, garlic, half the Emmental or Swiss cheese, and the milk. Pour the cheese mixture over the baked vegetables and sprinkle with the remaining Emmental or Swiss cheese. Reduce the oven temperature to at 300°F, and return the dish to the oven for another 30 minutes.

**Serve** with the reserved fennel leafy tops and parsley.

**For summer vegetable & herb frittata**, peel an extra-large zucchini, then halve and scoop out the seeds. Slice the flesh and toss in a bowl with 1½ tablespoons sea salt. Let stand for 20 minutes. Wash the zucchini in several changes of cold water to remove the salt and pat dry between paper towels. Melt 4 tablespoons butter in a skillet and gently sauté the zucchini, stirring frequently, for 10 minutes, until lightly brown. Stir in 2 teaspoons chopped savory and plenty of black pepper. Beat 6 eggs with ¼ cup light cream in a bowl and pour into the pan. Heat gently, pushing the mixture from the side of the pan into the center so that the uncooked eggs fill the space. Once the eggs start to set, cook gently for a few minutes, then transfer to a preheated moderate broiler and cook for about 5 minutes, until the surface is lightly browned and the filling is lightly set.

# kashmiri butternut squash curry

Serves **4**
Preparation time **20 minutes**
Cooking time **25 minutes**

2 **onions**, quartered
2 **garlic cloves**, peeled
1½ inch piece of **fresh ginger root**, peeled and sliced
1 large **red chile**, halved and seeded
1 teaspoon **cumin seeds**, coarsely crushed
1 teaspoon **coriander seeds**, coarsely crushed
5 **cardamom pods**, crushed
1 **butternut squash** or ½ **small pumpkin**, peeled and seeded
1 tablespoon **butter**
2 tablespoons **sunflower oil**
1 teaspoon **ground turmeric**
1 teaspoon **paprika**
1 **cinnamon stick**, halved
2 cups **vegetable stock** (see page 210)
⅔ cup **heavy cream**
⅓ cup coarsely chopped **pistachio nuts**
1 small bunch of **fresh cilantro**, torn
**salt** and **black pepper**

**Place** the onions, garlic, ginger, and chile in a food processor and process until finely chopped, or finely chop by hand. Mix with the crushed cumin, coriander, and cardamom.

**Slice** the squash or pumpkin into 1 inch wedges, then cut the wedges in half. Melt the butter with the oil in a large skillet and sauté the squash for 5 minutes, until lightly browned. Push the squash to one side of the pan, add the onion mixture, and sauté for about 5 minutes, until beginning to lightly brown.

**Add** the turmeric, paprika, and cinnamon to the skillet and cook briefly, then stir in the stock. Season to taste with salt and black pepper and bring to a boil. Reduce the heat, cover, and simmer for 10 minutes or until the squash is just cooked.

**Stir** in half the cream, half the pistachios, and half the cilantro leaves and gently heat through. Drizzle with the remaining cream and sprinkle with the remaining pistachios and cilantro, then serve with cooked rice and naans, if liked.

**For Kashmiri eggplant curry**, make the curry as above using 2 large eggplants, cut into 1½ inch cubes, in place of the pumpkin and adding 2 cups halved, trimmed green beans with the stock. Finish as above with the cream and cilantro but using ½ cup coarsely chopped blanched almonds instead of the pistachios.

# beet & goat cheese crisp

Serves **4**
Preparation time **25 minutes**
Cooking time **1½ hours**

16 **beets** (2 lb)
8 **small onions**, quartered
¼ cup **olive oil**
½ teaspoon **caraway seeds**
⅔ cup **all-purpose flour**
1 tablespoon chopped **lemon thyme**, plus extra to garnish
3 tablespoons **butter**, cut into small pieces
7 oz **soft goat cheese**, thinly sliced
**salt** and **black pepper**
**salad leaves**, to serve

**Scrub** the beets and cut into thin wedges. Put into a shallow ovenproof dish with the onions and drizzle with the oil. Sprinkle with the caraway seeds and season with a little salt and plenty of black pepper. Cook in a preheated oven, at 400°F, for about 1 hour, until the vegetables are roasted and tender, stirring once or twice during cooking.

**Meanwhile,** place the flour and lemon thyme in a bowl, add the butter, and rub in with the fingertips until the mixture resembles fine bread crumbs.

**Sprinkle** the goat cheese over the vegetables and sprinkle with the crumb mixture. Return to the oven for 25–30 minutes, until the topping is lightly browned. Sprinkle with thyme and serve with a leafy green salad, if liked.

**For roasted roots with horseradish crisp**, peel and cut 6 parsnips and 1 celeriac into small pieces and place in a shallow ovenproof dish with 3 small red onions, quartered. Drizzle with olive oil and cook in the oven as above. Prepare the crumb topping as above. Mix 1 cup light cream with 2 tablespoons hot horseradish sauce and pour the sauce over the roasted vegetables, then sprinkle with the crumb topping and bake as above.

# goat cheese & bell pepper lasagne

Serves **4**
Preparation time **20 minutes**
Cooking time **50 minutes – 1 hour**

- 6 **canned pimientos**
- 6 **tomatoes**, skinned (see page 11) and coarsely chopped
- 1 **yellow bell pepper**, cored, seeded and finely chopped
- 2 **zucchini**, thinly sliced
- 1⅓ cups thinly sliced **sun-dried tomatoes**
- ⅓ cup **sun-dried tomato pesto**
- 1 cup **basil**
- ¼ cup **olive oil**
- 5 oz **soft goat cheese**, crumbled
- 2½ cups store-bought or homemade **cheese sauce** (see below)
- 5 oz **dried egg lasagna noodles**
- ⅓ cup **grated Parmesan cheese**
- **salt** and **black pepper**
- **salad leaves**, to serve

**Drain** the pimientos and coarsely chop. Place in a bowl with the tomatoes, yellow bell pepper, zucchini, sun-dried tomatoes, and pesto. Tear the basil leaves and add to the bowl with the oil and a little salt and black pepper. Mix together thoroughly.

**Put** one-quarter of the tomato mixture into a 2-quart shallow ovenproof dish and dot with one-quarter of the goat cheese and ¼ cup of the cheese sauce. Cover with one-third of the lasagna noodles in a layer, breaking them to fit where necessary. Repeat the layering, finishing with a layer of the tomato mixture and goat cheese.

**Spoon** with the remaining cheese sauce and sprinkle with the Parmesan. Bake in a preheated oven, at 375°F, for 50 minutes–1 hour, until golden brown. Let stand for 10 minutes before serving with a leafy salad.

**For homemade cheese sauce**, put 2 cups milk in a saucepan with 1 small onion and 1 bay leaf. Heat until just boiling, then remove from the heat and let steep for 20 minutes. Strain the milk into a bowl. Melt 4 tablespoons butter in the cleaned saucepan, add ⅓ cup all-purpose flour, and stir in quickly. Cook over medium heat, stirring, for 1–2 minutes, then remove from the heat and gradually whisk in the steeped milk until blended. Return to the heat, bring gently to a boil, stirring, and cook for 2 minutes, until the sauce has thickened. Remove from the heat and stir in 1 cup shredded cheddar or Gruyère cheese until melted.

# beet & goat cheese risotto

Serves **4-6**
Preparation time **15 minutes**
Cooking time **40 minutes**

5 cups **vegetable stock**, (see page 210 for homemade)
6 **cooked beets**, drained (any juices reserved) and diced
¼ cup **extra virgin olive oil**
1 **red onion**, finely chopped
2 **garlic cloves**, crushed
2 teaspoons chopped **thyme,** plus extra to garnish
1½ cups **risotto rice**
½ cup **red wine**
4 oz **soft goat cheese**, diced
1 cup **pecans**, toasted and chopped
**salt** and **black pepper**
**salad leaves**, to serve

**Place** the stock and any reserved beet juices in a saucepan and bring to a gentle simmer.

**Meanwhile**, heat the oil in a separate saucepan and gently sauté the onion, garlic, and thyme with salt and black pepper to taste, stirring occasionally, for about 10 minutes, until the onion has softened but not browned.

**Add** the rice and cook, stirring, for 1 minute. Stir in the wine and cook quickly until the wine has been absorbed. Stir in the beets. Gradually add the hot stock to the pan, a ladleful at a time, and cook, stirring frequently, until each ladleful has mostly been absorbed before adding the next. This should take 20–25 minutes, by which time the rice should be tender but retaining a little bite and the consistency should be creamy. You may not need all the stock.

**Remove** the pan from the heat. Stir in the goat cheese and pecans, cover, and let stand for 2–3 minutes, until the cheese has melted. Garnish with extra thyme and serve with a leafy green salad.

**For beet & mascarpone risotto with pine nuts**, make the risotto as above, stirring in 5 oz mascarpone cheese in place of the goat cheese and sprinkling with pine nuts (about 1 tablespoon per portion) instead of adding the pecans.

# index

# acknowledgments

**Commissioning Editor:** Eleanor Maxfield
**Editor:** Jo Wilson
**Art Direction and Design:** Penny Stock
**Designer:** Eoghan O'Brien
**Stylist:** Kim Sullivan
**Photographer:** William Shaw
**Home Economist:** Joanna Farrow
**Picture Library Manager:** Jennifer Veall
**Copy-Editor:** Jo Richardson
**Proofreader:** Alison Bolus
**Indexer:** Diana LeCore
**Production Controller:** Sarah Kramer

**Special Photography:** © Octopus Publishing Group Limited/ William Shaw

**Other Photography:** © Octopus Publishing Group/167; Stephen Conroy 41, 57, 67, 85, 89, 103, 129, 147, 189, 203; Will Heap 125, 153; David Munns 49, 59; Lis Parsons 27, 229; William Shaw 197, 209, 225; Ian Wallace 16, 18, 79, 95, 109, 135, 185, 215.